TIME

Embracing Life's Fleeting Moment and Finding Meaning in the Passage of time

Ephraim Publishing

CONTENTS

FOREW ORD

It's rare to come across a book that speaks so eloquently to the delicate nature of our lives, a work that gently explores the rhythm of time and the profound effect it has on each of us. Moments Lost to Time is one such book, an exploration of the experiences that shape us, the memories that linger, and the quiet wisdom that arises which we learn to embrace the passage of time. Reading Moments Lost to Time feels like sitting down with a wise friend who understands the importance of living with awareness, cherishing what we have, and learning to let go. In a world that moves at breakneck speed, this book offers a rare invitation to slow down, to savor life's fleeting moments, and to reflect on what it means to live fully. Here, the reader is encouraged not only to understand time but to develop a relationship with it—one rooted in acceptance, gratitude, and appreciation.

The beauty of this book lies In its honesty about the challenges of living with time's ever-present flow. We all carry memories that bring both joy and sorrow, moments we long to revisit, and experiences we wish we could change. Yet Moments Lost to Time reminds us that life's impermanence is not a loss but a gift, a way of bringing depth and meaning to our existence. By reflecting on the advantages and disadvantages of time's passage, the book illuminates how each fleeting moment, whether filled with laughter or sorrow, is an opportunity to grow, learn, and become more fully ourselves. As you journey through these pages, you'll find yourself reflecting on your own life, on the experiences that have shaped you, and on the wisdom you've gathered along the way. You'll discover that time, while it may feel like a thief, is also a gentle teacher, guiding us to recognize what matters most. Moments Lost to Time is a tribute to this truth—a reminder that while we cannot hold onto everything, we can live fully in the present, carry forward the lessons of the past, and step into the future with open hearts. For anyone who has ever felt the pang of nostalgia, the weight of memory, or the desire to live more meaningfully, this book is a companion on that journey. It invites you to appreciate each moment as it comes, to let go when it's time, and to find peace in knowing that the essence of our experiences is never truly lost. As you turn these pages, may you find solace in the wisdom of time's passage, and may you feel inspired to live more deeply, with a heart that honors both what has been and what is yet to come. Moments Lost to Time is not only a book; it's an invitation to see life with fresh eyes, to celebrate the beauty within each fleeting moment, and to embrace the fullness of the journey.

INTRODUCTION

In Moments Lost to Time, we embark on an exploration of life's most delicate and universal truth: the passing of time. This book is an invitation to pause, reflect, and look deeper into the fleeting nature of our experiences—those moments that define us, shape us, and then quietly drift into memory. From moments of joy and love to times of sorrow and growth, each page of this book seeks to uncover the beauty hidden within life's transience. In a world that often urges us to cling to the present or dwell on the past, Moments Lost to Time challenges us to find peace in letting go, recognizing that the impermanence of each moment is what makes it precious. As we journey through its reflections, we discover that while time may take away, it also gives us gifts: resilience, wisdom, and an appreciation for the here and now. This book is for anyone who has felt the weight of nostalgia, the pang of regret, or the quiet beauty of a fleeting moment. It is for those seeking to live with greater awareness and gratitude, embracing each experience as it unfolds. In Moments Lost to Time, we learn to honor what has passed, cherish the present, and carry forward all that endures within us. Welcome to a journey that celebrates the depth and richness of our brief but meaningful moments. As you turn these pages, you'll be guided through reflections on memory, loss, and the delicate dance between HOLDING on and letting go. Moments Lost to Time will invite you to sit with both the joy and sorrow that accompany each passing moment, showing how these emotions are intertwined within us.

Rather than seeing time as something that takes away, we'll explore how time enriches our lives, transforming fleeting moments into lasting impressions that shape who we are. This journey will ask us to consider what it means to truly live in the present, to experience life with full awareness. It will challenge us to look back on our past not with regret or nostalgia but with gratitude for all that has brought us to this moment. As we explore the advantages and disadvantages of time's passage, we begin to see that life's brevity is not a limitation but a source of depth and meaning. Through gentle reflections, Moments Lost to Time will offer tools to help you embrace impermanence. You'll find words that resonate with your own story, reminding you of the beauty in every chapter, every fleeting encounter, and every lesson learned along the way. This book is not just about understanding time but about celebrating its gift. It encourages you to hold each moment, not with a tight grip, but with an open heart—allowing the journey to shape you and to bring a quiet sense of peace. Welcome to a journey through the timeless within the temporary. Moments Lost to Time will walk beside you as you honor the moments that have passed, cherish those yet to come, and find comfort in the enduring essence of your experiences.

PREFACE

Moments Lost to Time is a book born from the quiet reflections that accompany life's most fleeting experiences. Over the years, I've found myself wondering about the significance of time and the way it shapes each of us. How often do we experience something profound a glance, a sunset, a heartfelt conversation only to watch it fade into memory, impossible to relive but forever a part of us? This BOOK emerged as an attempt to honor those moments, to give voice to the intangible power they hold, and to explore how time relentless and constant deeply influences every chapter of our lives. At some point, we all come to realize that time is a companion that both gives and takes away. It grants us experiences, opportunities, and encounters, yet it never allows us to cling to them. Time is always in motion, urging us forward, often before we feel ready. The beauty of this truth, though difficult at first, lies in the understanding that each moment, no matter how brief, is valuable precisely because of its impermanence. In this way, time teaches us to appreciate what we have while we have it, to savor each day, and to find meaning in the ordinary moments that make up our lives. This book is both a tribute to those moments and a reflection on the journey of embracing impermanence. As I wrote, I found myself returning again and again to the tension we all feel between holding on and letting go. We want to preserve what we love, to capture the experiences that bring us joy or meaning. Yet, as each moment slips into the past, we are reminded that life is not something we can possess or control. Moments Lost to Time is a reminder that there is beauty in allowing life to flow, to let moments come and go, trusting that each experience leaves its mark on us, shaping us in ways that endure long after the moment itself has passed. Writing this book allowed me to delve into the nuances of memory, nostalgia, and acceptance. I reflected on the advantages of time's passage how it brings healing, wisdom, and perspective. Time has a way of transforming our experiences, turning what was once raw and immediate into something we can reflect upon with a sense of peace. The challenging moments that once felt insurmountable eventually soften, becoming lessons that guide us forward. At the same time, time reminds us of the limitations of memory; the details blur, the edges fade, and yet the essence remains. In this way, time both preserves and transforms our experiences, turning them into something we carry within us even as we move forward. I also explored the disadvantages of time's flow the inevitable sense of loss, the longing for moments that can never be reclaimed. There is a poignancy in knowing that we cannot hold onto everything, that certain experiences, people, and places will remain as memories. The ache of nostalgia and the pangs of regret are part of our shared humanity, and time's passing often brings them to the surface. Yet, I believe that these emotions, while challenging, hold valuable lessons. They remind us to live intentionally, to cherish what is present, and to recognize the power of each moment. In the end, the very fact that time takes away makes us more attuned to the beauty of what we have while it lasts.

THE ECHOES OF TIME

TIME
The Echoes that comes with time

Time isn't a river, nor a line, nor even the invisible passage we assume it to be. Time is an echo chamber, a resonance of past actions, whispers of the future, and the hum of possibilities present in every moment. Our story begins with Samuel, a man deeply attuned to these echoes, though he doesn't know it yet.

Samuel is an unassuming archivist in the city of Quiescence, where he spends his days cataloging remnants of forgotten history—letters that no longer reach their recipients, relics of wars that have faded into distant memories, voices recorded from past eras. As he ages, he becomes aware of faint echoes from beyond his own time—subtle, half-heard voices slipping through the creases in silence. They start out as murmurs, like the sound of wind passing through leaves. But as he listens more closely, Samuel realizes they are voices of people who lived long ago.

It begins on an evening like any other, as he sits in the dim light of his study, surrounded by papers and the soft glow of a single lamp. A faint, almost inaudible voice brushes against his consciousness, calling his name as if from a GREAT distance. Startled, Samuel listens, his heart racing, and he hears it again—a woman's voice, gentle yet firm, speaking of a place he doesn't know. Over the next few days, the whispers become more frequent, guiding him to a strange book buried in the archives: The Journal of Irina Lovaine, a figure lost to history.

The journal speaks of time not as a simple linear flow but as a fabric woven of many threads, each capable of slipping across boundaries, creating echoes that reverberate through generations. Samuel discovers that Irina, like himself, had the gift of hearing these echoes and used them to preserve not only history but the emotions, choices, and regrets of countless lives. Samuel's life begins to transform as he immerses himself in Irina's words, almost as though he's reliving her story in parallel.

Cover design by: Art Painter
Library of Congress
Printed in Nigeria

Days slip into weeks, and Samuel finds himself unable to sleep or focus on anything else. The voices grow louder, sometimes piercing the quiet of his evenings with vivid clarity. They speak not only in voices but in memories, images, entire scenes playing in his mind like lucid dreams. Through these visions, he witnesses moments of choice, pain, love, and loss from countless lives. He feels them as his own, understanding their decisions and heartbreaks. He becomes a vessel for these moments—a living, breathing testament to time's indelible touch on humanity.

One evening, as he falls deeper into the pull of the echoes, he meets the essence of Irina, not as a figure of the past but as a presence existing beyond the constraints of ordinary life. She reveals that he is not merely hearing echoes but is an echo himself, a continuation of a consciousness bound by a single, unyielding purpose: to bridge time's separated fragments, to bring forth connections lost to history.

Samuel is drawn to a place outside of Quiescence—a desolate hill where the remnants of an ancient stone circle stand under the wide, dark sky. Here, the echoes are strongest, the air thick with whispers from all ages. Irina's voice is clearest here, and she tells him that the world is reaching a moment of reckoning, where the past and future collide. Samuel's task is to bear witness, to weave the voices he has heard intoIt begins on an evening like any other, with Samuel sitting alone in the dimly lit back room of the Quiescence Archive. The soft, warm glow of his desk lamp pools over old, brittle papers, casting shadows that dance across the walls. That night, he's been reading a letter written by a soldier in a forgotten war. The letter is frayed and stained, and the ink has faded to a ghostly hue. As Samuel reads, he feels a peculiar tug, as though some unseen force pulls him deeper into the words, the story, the emotions that linger on the page.

The letter is addressed to a woman named Elise, and the soldier writes about their plans to meet again when the war is over, of the life they'll build together, the places they'll visit. His words are filled with longing, but also a curious resignation, as though he already knows that these dreams will never come to pass.

Suddenly, the room feels colder, and a strange, whispering echo fills Samuel's ears. It's faint at first, barely more than a rustling, but as he listens, it begins to resolve into words—a voice, worn and soft, as though it's traveled a great distance through the shadows of time.

"...find her... tell Elise... not to wait..."

The words linger in the air, and Samuel sits frozen, unsure if he's heard them at all. But the sensation stays with him, hanging like a chill in his bones. He tries to shake it off, tells himself it's just his imagination, maybe the wind seeping through the cracks in the old building. Yet as he listens, he realizes it wasn't the sound of wind. It was the unmistakable tone of a voice calling to him from beyond the edges of his world.

Over the following weeks, the strange occurrences multiply. The faint echoes come more frequently, slipping into his reality at odd moments—when he's shelving books, reading an old newspaper, or simply walking home at night. They aren't always clear; often, they're just murmurs, fragments of forgotten conversations or snippets of laughter. But every now and then, he catches glimpses of something more—a name, a place, a fleeting emotion that's not his own.

One evening, as he's working late, Samuel hears the voice again, clearer this time. "Find her," it urges, with a desperate edge he can't ignore. "Tell her not to wait..." The voice fades, but something lingers in the silence, something that feels like a plea.

Against his better judgment, Samuel begins to investigate the origins of the letter. He digs through military records, census documents, old newspapers—anything that might offer a clue. Days blur into nights, and he loses himself in the hunt, following one tenuous lead after another. He feels as though he's peeling back layers of time, uncovering fragments of forgotten lives and stories that have been buried in dust and silence.

Through his research, he discovers that the soldier was named Thomas Grey, a young man who disappeared during a battle, presumed lost. Elise, the woman he wrote to, had waited years for him, holding onto hope long after everyone else had given up. She never married, never moved on, but stayed in the small town where they had planned to start their life together.

Samuel feels an ache for Elise, a woman he's never met, who's long since passed from the world of the living. He becomes consumed by the need to bridge the gap between them, to find some way of delivering Thomas's message across the impossible chasm of time.

One night, as he's pouring over an old journal written by Elise herself, Samuel falls asleep in the archives. He dreams of a field bathed in soft moonlight, with wildflowers swaying in a gentle breeze. In the distance, he sees a figure—a woman with dark hair, her face turned away, looking toward the horizon. He knows instinctively that it's Elise. He calls her name, but she doesn't turn. Instead, she stands there, still as a statue, her posture heavy with waiting.

When he wakes, the weight of the dream lingers, pressing on his chest. He realizes he can't simply let this go. There's something about Elise's waiting, her faithfulness to a promise made in a world that no longer exists, that speaks to him in a way he can't explain. He feels a strange kinship with her, as though they are bound together by invisible threads stretching through the years.

Over the coming days, Samuel finds himself slipping into what he can only describe as a trance, where the line between past and present grows thin. He catches glimpses of Elise's life—moments of her sitting by the window, a candle burning as she waits through the night, her hands clutching a faded letter. He sees her wandering through the fields near her home, her eyes searching the horizon, her heart forever suspended in that place between hope and despair.

The echoes grow stronger, and Samuel feels as though he's falling through layers of reality, spiraling deeper into a world that isn't his own. One night, he decides to return to the field from his dream. It's a wild place on the outskirts of town, where the land stretches open under a vast, star-filled sky. He stands there, listening to the silence, letting the weight of the past settle around him.

As he stands in the field, he hears the voice again, clearer than ever. "Tell her... I'm here." The words are laced with a quiet sorrow, but also a sense of peace, as though the speaker has finally come to rest. Samuel feels an overwhelming need to respond, to offer some acknowledgment of the message.

"I'll find her," he whispers, though he doesn't know who he's speaking to or how he'll keep the promise. But in that moment, he feels a warmth radiate through him, a sense of completion that fills the hollow ache in his chest.

From that night forward, Samuel begins to change. He's no longer merely an archivist cataloging dusty relics; he becomes a bridge, a conduit for the echoes of time. People in the town start to notice his transformation, the way he seems to carry a piece of the past with him, a kind of otherworldly presence that sets him apart. Some avoid him, unsettled by the change, but others are drawn to him, sensing in him a depth and wisdom that transcends the ordinary flow of time.

Years pass, and Samuel continues his work, helping others to connect with the echoes of their own pasts. He becomes a keeper of lost stories, a guardian of the forgotten, and a silent witness to the lives that once filled the world. He never finds Elise in the way he had hoped, but in some unspoken way, he feels that she is with him, a quiet presence that lingers on the edges of his awareness, her waiting finally come to an end.

In the final years of his life, Samuel sits alone in the Quiescence Archive, his hair silver and his eyes clouded with age. The voices still whisper to him, softer now, but no less insistent, as he closes his eyes for the last time.

he feels a warmth around him, a sense of peace that fills every corner of his being. And in that moment, he knows that he has fulfilled his purpose—that he has carried the echoes of time forward, weaving them into the fabric of the present, so that the past will never be truly forgotten.

In the stillness, he hears the faintest of voices, as though coming from a ~~*place far beyond the veil of death. "Thank you," it says, a whisper that resonates with gratitude and love. And as he slips into the silence, Samuel realizes that he, too, has become an echo, a quiet reverberation of all the lives he touched, all the stories he preserved.*~~

Time isn't a river, nor a line, nor even the passage we assume it to be. Time ~~*is an echo—a memory that lingers, a whisper that we carry forward, a resonance that never truly fades.*~~

~~*As Samuel's spirit slips into the vast, unknowable realm beyond, the Quiescence Archive remains, a repository of stories still humming with the echoes he once felt so deeply. And yet, his presence lingers within its walls, woven into the very structure, like a faint warmth left in a room after the fire has died down. It is said by those who work in the Archive long after him that they can sometimes feel him—a comforting presence, a silent guardian watching over the forgotten relics, urging the living to listen to what remains.*~~

Years go by, and generations of archivists come and go, each leaving their own imprint, yet no one quite as attuned to the whispers of time as Samuel. The Archive's collection grows, filling with more voices of the lost and the overlooked, histories of wars and peace, love and sorrow. But one day, a young woman named Lena arrives to take over the role of chief archivist. Lena is quiet, observant, and—though she doesn't realize it at first—curiously in tune with the strange energy that permeates the Archive.

In the early weeks of her new job, Lena begins to feel a subtle presence. There are moments, especially late at night when the rest of the staff has gone, that she senses she is not alone. At first, she dismisses it as her imagination or the remnants of a long day, but the feeling grows stronger with time. One night, as she's organizing a set of journals from the early 20th century, she hears what sounds like a faint sigh, barely more than a breath, slipping through the stillness.

She pauses, her hands frozen over the pages, her heart racing. It's not fear that holds her—it's a strange mixture of awe and curiosity, an instinctive knowing that something beyond her understanding is reaching out. She closes her eyes and listens, just as Samuel once did, tuning into the silence until she hears it again—a soft, whispering voice, as though spoken from a place where words themselves are fragile and ephemeral.

"Listen," it says. "Do not let them be forgotten."

The words linger in her mind, filling her with a sense of purpose she hadn't fully understood until that moment. She doesn't know whose voice it is, but she feels a deep kinship with it, as though the voice belongs to someone who has waited a long time to be heard. Lena, moved by the experience, resolves to delve deeper into the stories within the Archive, to uncover not just names and dates, but the hidden lives and emotions woven into each item she touches.

As the years pass, Lena develops her own way of working with the echoes. She starts writing the stories she hears into a journal of her own, carefully documenting every fragment, every whisper, every trace of a life that flickers through her awareness. It becomes a kind of ritual, a communion with the past that connects her to something larger, something timeless. She learns that she can feel the echoes more strongly if she lets herself slip into a meditative state, emptying her mind until she becomes a vessel for the voices waiting just beyond the veil.

One night, as she sits alone in the Archive, she feels a presence stronger than any she's felt before—a gentle but insistent pull that leads her to a dusty, forgotten corner of the Archive. She finds herself standing before a drawer she's never noticed, hidden away behind a stack of old shelves. Inside, she finds a leather-bound journal with pages yellowed by age, the ink faded but still legible.

She opens it, and her breath catches as she reads the first entry: it's Samuel's handwriting, his personal journal. He writes about the echoes he heard, the strange sensation of lives intersecting through the folds of time, the pull he felt to connect the lost voices with the present. The entries are filled with his reflections, his frustrations, and ultimately, his acceptance of his role as a bridge between worlds. Lena reads for hours, captivated by his words, his journey, and his insights.

Then she comes to the final entry. It is brief, a single line that reads, "Time is an echo, a resonance that lives within us all." As she reads these words, she feels a deep, inexplicable connection, as though Samuel himself is standing beside her, watching over her work, guiding her. She realizes that she is not alone in her calling—that she, too, has become a custodian of these echoes, a guardian of the forgotten.

Days turn into years, and Lena becomes known in the town as the woman who listens to the past. People bring her items they've inherited but do not understand—a locket with a photo of a woman no one can identify, a letter with no return address, a diary filled with confessions

People bring her items they've inherited but do not understand—a locket with a photo of a woman no one can identify, a letter with no return address, a diary filled with confessions and regrets. They come seeking closure, hoping Lena can hear what remains unsaid, connect them with the hidden stories of those who came before. She listens carefully, taking each item into her hands, allowing herself to become immersed in its history, waiting for the soft hum of memory to reveal itself.

One evening, a young man named Emmett arrives, clutching an old pocket watch with initials engraved on the back: "T.G." His eyes are haunted, his voice hesitant as he explains that he inherited it from his grandfather, who had never explained where it came from or to whom it had once belonged. Emmett had grown up with stories of a mysterious great-uncle who had vanished in the war, but his family rarely spoke of him. “They say he left a woman waiting,” Emmett whispers, as if afraid of disturbing the watch itself.

Lena holds the watch delicately, feeling its cold metal press into her palm, and immediately senses a familiar vibration within it, as though it holds echoes of a story she has heard before. She concentrates, letting herself slip into the stillness, until faint images begin to form—a young soldier writing a letter, his hand shaking as he tries to express feelings that words can scarcely hold. The letter is to a woman named Elise, and the grief and urgency in his heart are palpable.

Lena’s own heart clenches as she realizes this must be Thomas Grey, the soldier from Samuel’s journal, the man who had called out across time with his message for Elise. She feels as if she’s uncovered a thread that Samuel himself had been trying to follow, a story that had remained unfinished. With tears in her eyes, she looks up at Emmett, who’s watching her with bated breath.

“Your great-uncle was Thomas Grey,” she says softly. “He loved a woman named Elise, and he left this world with words unspoken, hoping someone would remember.” She pauses, feeling the weight of the story settling between them. “He didn’t want her to wait in vain, but she did. She waited for him, long after everyone else had moved on.”

Emmett’s face crumples with a mixture of sadness and relief, as though a burden he’d carried unknowingly has finally been lifted. “I wish I could tell her he tried to come back,” he murmurs. “I wish I could give her peace.”

Lena places a comforting hand on his arm. “Perhaps, in some way, you have,” she says. “These echoes, they ripple through time. I think she feels it, wherever she is now.”

After Emmett leaves, Lena sits alone, feeling the quiet around her, the gentle hum of memories lingering in the room. She understands now that she is part of a chain, a series of connections stretching through generations, each person touched by the past, each becoming a part of the echo. Samuel, Thomas, Elise, and now Emmett—they are all woven Into this vast tapestry, a resonance that binds their lives to each other.

In the years that follow, Lena dedicates herself to the Archive with even greater purpose, continuing Samuel's work, bridging lives separated by the years. She becomes a master at listening, uncovering layers of stories, finding closure for those who seek it, and peace for those who have passed. Through her, forgotten voices are brought back to life, given the dignity of being remembered, and the echoes grow richer, stronger, until the very walls of the Archive seem to pulse with a life of their own.

Eventually, Lena's time, too, begins to draw to a close. She knows that she will soon leave the world she has guarded so faithfully, and though there is sadness, there is also a deep sense of fulfillment. She has carried Samuel's work forward, has honored the voices that whispered through her life, and she knows that someone else will come after her, another keeper of the echoes.

One cold winter's night, as she sits alone in the Archive, Lena closes her eyes and listens one last time. The whispers come, gentle and warm, like a final embrace. Among them, she hears Samuel's voice, soft and clear: "Thank you, Lena. You carried the echoes well."

A smile touches her lips as she lets go, her spirit slipping into the endless resonance of time, joining the chorus of those who came before. And as she departs, she becomes one of the whispers in the Archive, a quiet but enduring presence, guiding future archivists toward the stories waiting to be heard.

The Quiescence Archive remains, a sanctuary of memories, a bridge between past and present, where echoes will continue to whisper, and guardians will rise to listen. And somewhere beyond time itself, the voices of Samuel, Lena, Thomas, Elise, and countless others linger, carried forward, resonating eternally, their stories a gentle reminder that time itself is but an echo—one that will never fade.

After Lena's passing, the Quiescence Archive enters a period of quiet. For months, it sits undisturbed, the dust settling on rows of shelves and the collection waiting in a kind of patient silence. Yet, the energy remains, woven into the Archive's very foundation—a palpable hum that the rare visitors feel as soon as they enter, an atmosphere thick with the weight of stories untold.

When the town council finally appoints a new archivist, it chooses someone who seems entirely unlike Samuel or Lena. The new keeper is a young woman named Mira, who approaches the position with a pragmatic, almost detached perspective. To her, it's just a job—a responsibility she's taken to make ends meet, not an invitation to explore the mysteries of time. She begins her work methodically, cataloging items with efficiency, organizing the shelves, and meticulously dusting and restoring the books. For Mira, the Archive is merely an old building filled with relics, the ghosts of a past that no longer matters.

But even Mira cannot escape the peculiar aura that lingers in the Quiescence ~~Archive. Over time, she begins to notice odd things—the faint scent of lavender when she's alone at her desk, a gentle rustling of paper when no one else is around, and occasionally, the unmistakable sensation of someone standing just over her shoulder, watching her work. She dismisses it as her imagination, a quirk of an old building, but deep down, a part of her senses that there is something more—a pulse, a presence woven into the very fabric of the Archive~~.

One evening, after a particularly long day of work, Mira finds herself drawn to the same corner where Lena had once discovered Samuel's journal. She hesitates, unsure of why she feels compelled to search there, but something tugs at her, a quiet insistence that she can't ignore. She opens the drawer and finds, not a journal this time, but an old, dusty box tied with a frayed ribbon.

Inside, she finds letters—dozens of them—each in an envelope marked with a name she doesn't recognize, each letter bearing a date from decades ago. The handwriting varies, and yet, as she reads through them, a theme emerges: people writing to loved ones they've lost, messages they'd hoped would somehow reach across time and distance. The letters are filled with words unsaid, apologies never spoken, hopes and promises left unfulfilled.

As Mira reads, a strange warmth spreads through her, and a quiet voice in her mind whispers, Listen. She pauses, closing her eyes, and for the first time, she allows herself to truly listen, as though some part of her is waking up, tapping into something greater than herself. A single, faint voice emerges from the silence, its tone gentle and familiar.

"Tell them... tell them they're not alone."

Mira opens her eyes, her heart racing. She feels as though she's been given a glimpse into something vast, something that stretches far beyond her own life. She senses the presence of those who had come before her—Samuel, Lena, and countless others whose voices linger in the Archive, bound together by the same thread of memory and purpose.

The sensation Is overwhelming, filling her with an inexplicable reverence, and she realizes that she has become a part of this chain, that she, too, is a keeper of the echoes. It's as though the Archive itself has chosen her, reaching out across time to draw her into its fold. And for the first time, Mira understands the true purpose of her work—not simply to organize artifacts, but to honor the voices that still reside within them, to be a bridge for those whose stories remain incomplete.

From that moment on, Mira approaches her work with a new sense of reverence. She takes the time to listen to each item, to feel its history, allowing herself to become attuned to the whispers and echoes that linger. She learns to recognize the subtle cues—the faint scent of perfume that accompanies a love letter, the weight of sorrow that hangs around an old photograph, the pang of regret embedded in an unfinished letter. Each item becomes a doorway, a window into a life that once was, and she allows herself to honor each story, however brief or fragmented.

Word begins to spread around town of Mira's ability to connect people with their family histories, to help them understand the stories behind the objects they bring her. People come to her with old photographs, diaries, trinkets they don't understand, and she listens to them, treating each piece with a quiet respect. She becomes a confidante, a trusted keeper of family secrets and unsolved mysteries, gently helping others find peace in the stories that l i nge r.

And as Mira delves deeper into the lives of those who left their traces behind, she realizes that she, too, is leaving her own echo. She feels it with each passing day—a resonance within the Archive, as though her very presence has become woven into the building, into its memory. She understands now what Samuel and Lena had come to know—that time is not something that simply moves forward, leaving the past behind, but something that circles, that echoes, that weaves itself into each life, each generation, in ways that defy logic or explanation.

Years later, when Mira grows old and her own time in the Archive draws to a close, she feels a sense of fulfillment, a peaceful acceptance of the role she has played. She knows that her own echo will remain, that the Archive will remember her, just as it remembers those who came before.

On her last day, as she closes the doors of the Archive one final time, she turns to the empty shelves, the shadowed corridors, and the countless relics of forgotten lives. She smiles, her voice soft but steady as she whispers, "Thank you for letting me listen."

And as she steps away, she leaves behind a presence, a warmth that joins the echoes within the Archive, becoming a part of the ever-growing resonance of stories that will continue long after she is gone. The Archive remains, a sanctuary of memory, a place where time is not linear, but circular, eternal—an echo that reverberates endlessly, carrying forward the lives, the loves, the dreams of those*who once walked this earth, ensuring that they will never be truly forgotten.*

And somewhere, deep within the heart of the Archive, the faintest of voices lingers, whispering into the silence, waiting patiently for the next listener, the next keeper, to answer its call.

THROUGH THE SANDS OF TIME

TIME
Walking on time as sands

In a world woven together by the threads of time, every sound carries a memory, a whisper of the past that resonates through the ages. It is in these echoes that we find our inspiration, a call to understand the depth of our existence and the stories that have shaped humanity. Each moment, fleeting and yet eternal, is a testament to our collective journey, reminding us that we are part of something much greater than ourselves.

Imagine standing in a quiet place, perhaps beneath the sprawling branches of an ancient tree, where the winds carry the laughter of children who played long ago. Every rustle of the leaves tells a tale, a fragment of history captured in sound. It is here, in this serene space, that we can pause and listen to the symphony of life surrounding us.

As we delve into the sounds of time, we are reminded that each of us is a keeper of stories. The voices of our ancestors, the whispers of those who walked before us, echo in our hearts. They remind us of resilience in the face of adversity, love that transcends generations, and dreams that inspire courage. In their stories, we find our own narratives—our joys, our struggles, our triumphs.

Consider the sound of a distant bell ringing, resonating across a village. It marks not only the passage of time but also the gathering of community. It reminds us of our interconnectedness, of how we are woven into the fabric of those around us. Each bell toll signifies a moment shared, a memory created, a life lived in the embrace of others. It inspires us to cherish the connections we forge, to nurture the bonds that tie us together, for they are the lifeblood of our existence.

In the hustle and bustle of modern life, it is easy to become disconnected from these echoes. The clamor of technology, the rush of daily responsibilities can drown out the soft whispers of the past. Yet, if we take a moment to still our minds and listen, we can hear the gentle reminder of our history—a reminder to honor where we come from and to recognize the footprints we leave behind.

Let us be inspired by the sounds of time, allowing them to guide our actions and choices. When we hear the laughter of children, let it inspire us to nurture the innocence and joy that still resides within us. When we hear the weeping of a sorrowful song, let it remind us to embrace our vulnerability and to extend compassion to others. When we hear the rustling of pages in a book, let it remind us of the wisdom waiting to be discovered, the lessons from the past that can illuminate our present.

As we walk through life, may we remember to listen—to the stories whispered in the winds, to the songs sung in the night, to the silence that speaks volumes. The echoes of time are not merely relics of history; they are a source of inspiration, urging us to live authentically, to love deeply, and to dream boldly. They remind us that we are part of an intricate tapestry woven from countless threads of experience, and in this tapestry, we each hold a unique place.

In the end, it is through the sounds of time that we find our purpose. We are not just individuals moving through space; we are echoes of those who came before us, and we are also the voices for those yet to come. Each moment is an opportunity to contribute to the symphony of existence, to add our notes to the harmonious blend of life.

So let us embrace the sounds of time, allowing them to inspire us, to connect us, and to guide us. Let us celebrate our shared humanity, for in doing so, we not only honor the past but also illuminate the path forward. As we listen, may we find strength in our stories, courage in our connections, and beauty in the echoes of our shared journey.

Through the Sounds of Time (Continued)

As we embark on our journeys, let us also recognize the profound power of silence. In the quiet moments, we often discover the deepest truths. It is within silence that we can truly listen—not only to the world around us but also to the whispers of our own hearts. It is a space where inspiration can flourish, where ideas can take root, and where our innermost selves can emerge unfiltered. Embracing silence allows us to reflect, to ponder, and to connect with our essence.

Imagine standing at the edge of a serene lake, its surface mirroring the sky, perfectly still. The only sounds are the gentle lapping of the water and the distant calls of birds. In this tranquility, one can hear the echoes of their thoughts, their hopes, and their dreams. It is here that inspiration strikes, urging us to pursue our passions, to take risks, and to forge our paths, unencumbered by the noise of external expectations.

In this journey through time and sound, we must also remember the importance of sharing our stories. Each of us carries within us a wealth of experiences that shape our perspectives and inform our decisions. When we share our stories, we invite others into our worlds, fostering connection and understanding. It is in the act of storytelling that we can heal, inspire, and empower one another.

Consider the power of a simple conversation. When we listen to someone share their experiences—their struggles, their triumphs, their lessons—we create a space for empathy and compassion. We find common ground in our shared humanity. Through these exchanges, we break down barriers, dispel isolation, and cultivate a sense of belonging.

We can also find inspiration in the stories of those who came before us—figures in history whose lives resonate with courage and resilience. Think of the poets, artists, and leaders who have used their voices to inspire change. Their echoes still ring in our ears, encouraging us to stand for what we believe in, to pursue our dreams with fervor, and to strive for a better world. They remind us that our voices matter and that we have the power to create ripples of change, just as they did.

As we navigate the complexities of life, let us also be attuned to the lessons that nature offers. The sounds of the earth—rustling leaves, flowing rivers, and the songs of birds—carry wisdom that transcends time. They remind us of the cycles of life, the beauty of growth, and the inevitability of change. Nature teaches us to be present, to appreciate the fleeting moments, and to embrace the impermanence of existence.

In the gentle sway of a tree, we find resilience. In the rhythm of the ocean's waves, we discover the power of renewal. Nature speaks in a language that transcends words, encouraging us to find harmony within ourselves and with the world around us. When we immerse ourselves in the sounds of nature, we reconnect with the essence of life itself, igniting our creativity and inspiring us to take action.

Let us also not forget the importance of gratitude in our journey through the sounds of time. When we cultivate an attitude of gratitude, we open our hearts to the beauty that surrounds us. We learn to appreciate the small moments—the laughter of a friend, the warmth of the sun, the comfort of a familiar song. In these moments, we find inspiration to create, to express, and to share our gifts with the world.

Gratitude allows us to acknowledge the connections we have forged, the lessons we have learned, and the beauty that exists even amidst challenges. It inspires us to be more present, to engage more fully in our lives, and to recognize the richness of the tapestry we are weaving. When we approach life with gratitude, we transform our perspectives, igniting a spark of inspiration that propels us forward.

As we reflect on the sounds of time, let us remember that we are not alone in our journeys. We are part of a vast web of interconnected stories, each thread contributing to the larger narrative of humanity. Through our shared experiences, we can uplift one another, celebrating our victories and supporting one another in times of need.

In the end, the sounds of time invite us to live fully, to embrace our voices, and to weave our stories into the collective tapestry of existence. They remind us that each moment is a gift, each experience a chapter in our personal and communal narratives. As we listen to the echoes of the past and the melodies of the present, may we find inspiration to create a future filled with hope, compassion, and connection.

So let us journey forward, with open hearts and open minds, ready to listen and to learn. Let us celebrate the beauty of our shared humanity, finding strength in our stories and inspiration in the echoes of time. For in this symphony of life, we are all musicians, each playing our unique note, creating a harmonious blend that resonates through the ages. Together, let us make music that transcends time, a melody of love, resilience, and inspiration that will echo through generations to come.

Through the Sounds of Time (Continued)

As we stand on the threshold of our lives, we must recognize that the echoes of time serve not only as reminders of where we've been but also as guiding lights for where we are going. Each sound—a laugh, a sigh, a whisper—holds within it a lesson waiting to be uncovered. In the tapestry of our experiences, these sounds invite us to reflect on our choices and inspire us to act with intention and purpose.

Consider the soft murmur of a stream as it flows through a quiet forest. This sound, soothing and constant, serves as a reminder that life, much like water, finds its own path. It teaches us that even in the face of obstacles, we can adapt and flow. When we encounter challenges, we can choose to resist or, like the water, bend and shape ourselves to navigate around them. The stream's journey is a testament to resilience, urging us to be flexible in our pursuits and to embrace change as a natural part of life.

In the cacophony of urban life, the sounds of laughter, conversation, and music mingle, creating a rich tapestry of human experience. These sounds inspire us to seek connection and community. They remind us that we are all part of a larger narrative, each voice contributing to the symphony of life. When we hear a child's laughter, it ignites joy within us; when we hear a friend's encouraging words, it fills us with hope. These interactions remind us of the importance of being present, of engaging with those around us, and of celebrating the moments we share.

The sounds of time also teach us the value of patience. Like the gentle ticking of a clock, we are reminded that every moment has its place. In a world that often demands instant results, the rhythmic ticking encourages us to embrace the process rather than rush toward the outcome. Each tick is a reminder that time unfolds in its own way, and within that unfolding lies growth and discovery. When we practice patience, we cultivate the ability to listen deeply—to ourselves, to others, and to the world.

Every heartbeat is a sound that resonates within us, a reminder of our aliveness. It is a call to action, urging us to pursue our passions and to live fully. When we take a moment to feel our heartbeat, we reconnect with our essence, acknowledging the gift of life itself. This awareness inspires us to seek out what brings us joy, to embrace our dreams, and to take bold steps toward our aspirations. We become aware that the time we have is precious and that we must make the most of every heartbeat.

As we reflect on the lessons that the sounds of time impart, let us also honor the importance of mindfulness. In our fast-paced world, we often forget to pause and simply listen. Mindfulness invites us to be present in the moment, to engage with our surroundings fully, and to appreciate the beauty that lies within the ordinary. When we practice mindfulness, we become attuned to the sounds around us—the rustling leaves, the chirping birds, the soft hum of life. These sounds ground us, reminding us that we are part of a larger ecosystem, intricately connected to the earth and to one another.

In the stillness of mindfulness, we find inspiration to create. The act of creation—whether through art, writing, music, or any other form—allows us to express our unique voices and contribute to the world's rich tapestry.

When we create, we translate the sounds of our experiences into something tangible, allowing others to connect with our stories and emotions. This sharing of creativity not only enriches our own lives but also inspires others to find and express their own voices.

Let us also recognize the importance of reflection as we journey through the sounds of time. In our busy lives, it is easy to overlook the lessons learned from past experiences. By taking time to reflect, we can gain insights into our journeys, understanding what has shaped us and what we wish to carry forward. Reflection allows us to learn from our mistakes and celebrate our successes, deepening our understanding of ourselves and our purpose.

When we sit in quiet contemplation, we can hear the echoes of our past experiences—both the joyful moments that make our hearts sing and the painful memories that have taught us resilience. It is in this reflection that we find clarity, understanding our desires and aspirations more profoundly. The sounds of time become a compass, guiding us toward our true north and inspiring us to pursue our passions with renewed vigor.

As we embrace the sounds of time, let us also foster a spirit of gratitude. Gratitude shifts our perspective, allowing us to appreciate the abundance that surrounds us. When we express gratitude, we open our hearts to the beauty of life—the warmth of the sun on our skin, the kindness of a stranger, the love of family and friends. Each moment of gratitude is a note in the symphony of our lives, enriching our experiences and inspiring us to spread positivity.

In our relationships, gratitude fosters deeper connections. When we take the time to acknowledge the people who impact our lives—those who lift us up, challenge us, and inspire us—we cultivate a culture of appreciation. Sharing our gratitude creates an environment of love and support, where everyone feels valued and heard. In this way, the sounds of time resonate through our interactions, creating a harmonious community rooted in understanding and compassion.

Finally, let us not forget that the sounds of time extend beyond our individual experiences; they encompass the broader human experience. As we listen to the stories of those from different cultures, backgrounds, and walks of life, we expand our understanding of the world. These diverse perspectives enrich our lives, allowing us to appreciate the beautiful complexity of huma ni ty.

In hearing the voices of others, we develop empathy, understanding that every person carries their own burdens and joys. Each story adds depth to the collective narrative, reminding us that we are not alone in our struggles. By listening to one another, we weave a rich tapestry of shared experiences that transcends borders and differences.

As we move forward, may we carry the echoes of time with us—allowing them to inspire, guide, and connect us. Let us be active listeners, embracing the sounds of the world around us and within us. In doing so, we unlock the potential to create, to love, and to grow, enriching not only our lives but the lives of those we encounter.

In conclusion, the sounds of time are a powerful force, reminding us of our shared humanity and the beauty of existence. They invite us to listen deeply, to reflect on our journeys, and to embrace our voices. As we navigate the complexities of life, let us honor the echoes of our past, celebrate the present, and inspire one another to shape a future filled with compassion, creativity, and connection. May the sounds of time continue to resonate within us, guiding us on our paths and inspiring us to leave a lasting impact on the world. Together, let us create a symphony of life that echoes through the ages, a testament to the power of the human spirit.

Time is both infinite and limited, elusive and ever-present. When we speak of "borrowed time," we acknowledge the fragile nature of existence, the fleeting moments that define our lives, and the paradox of experiencing time as something both immense and intimate. This exploration considers time as a mysterious force, unfathomable yet defining, a continuum that we navigate within our brief, bounded lives. Our lives, in their brevity, unfold as episodes of "borrowed time"—moments that are neither owned nor fully understood but are experienced deeply.

Time, in its essence, is neither friend nor foe. It is a silent witness, indifferent to the beings that occupy it. It exists as a backdrop, yet its very passage transforms the universe. For us, time is measured, dissected, and understood through clocks and calendars, yet the mystery of what it is persists. In our minds, we fragment it into units of seconds, minutes, days, and years, attempting to capture something that slips away the moment it is perceived.

When we view time as something borrowed, we recognize that it does not belong to us, no matter how hard we try to contain it. The minutes and hours that we think of as "ours" are simply moments loaned to us, fleeting intervals that we can only inhabit temporarily. Time, in this sense, is an eternal flow, and our lives merely ripple within it.

Time moves forward with a force that is irreversible. The past, once gone, exists only as memory, and the future as a realm of possibility. Yet, each moment arrives as if on loan, carrying within it a fleeting chance to be fully lived. There is an urgency to borrowed time, an awareness that it is ephemeral, and this impermanence often gives rise to both beauty and tragedy. We spend our lives racing to capture moments before they dissolve, living in awareness that they are never truly ours.

This fleetingness defines human experience. Whether in moments of joy or sorrow, in the heights of love or in the depths of despair, the awareness of time's transitory nature amplifies every sensation. The urgency we feel is not an illusion—it is an understanding that life, at its core, is brief. Borrowed time means that each experience, no matter how intense, will soon fade, making way for what comes next.

Time is both a gift and a burden. On one hand, knowing that it is borrowed can inspire us to live fully, to take chances, and to experience life without hesitation. The knowledge that time is limited can free us from the constraints of fear, allowing us to live courageously, knowing that there is no endless tomorrow. To live as though each day could be the last is to embrace time's finite nature with a sense of liberation, using it to fuel creativity, exploration, and self-discovery.

On the other hand, time as a borrowed commodity imposes limits. We are bound by the hours of each day, the weeks of each year, the decades of a life. Our dreams, aspirations, and plans all exist within this boundary, creating an unspoken pressure to achieve, to grow, to accomplish before time "runs out." This constraint shapes human behavior in countless ways, from the pursuit of success to the cultivation of relationships, as we strive to make the most of the time we have.

Although time moves in a linear fashion, human perception often finds comfort in cycles—the recurring patterns of days, months, seasons, and years. These cycles give the illusion of permanence within the flow of borrowed time, creating a rhythm that we can navigate. We structure our lives around these rhythms, celebrating the return of spring, the passing of a year, the anniversary of milestones. These cycles offer a sense of stability, an anchor in the river of time, even as they remind us of its passage.

Yet, each cycle is unique; no two springs, summers, or years are identical. As much as the cycles comfort us, they also reveal the gradual change within us and around us. Each repetition contains subtle transformations, a reminder that even within the framework of familiar patterns, we are moving ever forward, borrowing time from an unseen source.

Nature offers a powerful metaphor for borrowed time. The life cycle of a tree, the migration of birds, the changing tides—each of these reflects time's impact on existence. In nature, nothing is permanent; growth, decay, and renewal are constants. Trees lose their leaves, only to grow them anew; rivers flow, only to reach the sea. This natural progression is a reminder that life, too, follows a cycle of beginnings and endings.

In the natural world, there is no illusion of ownership over time. Each season unfolds as it must, each creature lives and dies within a larger ecosystem. In this, nature embodies the acceptance of borrowed time, showing us how to live with grace within the boundaries we are given.

For humans, the awareness of time's finite nature often leads to a desire for legacy—a wish to leave something behind that will endure beyond our own lifespan. Borrowed time drives us to create, to contribute, to build, in the hope that our actions will have a lasting impact. Whether through art, knowledge, or family, the pursuit of legacy is an attempt to extend our reach into a future we will not see.

This desire for legacy is both a product of and a response to borrowed time. In creating something that endures, we seek to transcend the limitations of our brief existence, to leave a trace of ourselves that will linger even after we are gone. It is a form of resistance against the impermanence of life, a way of transforming borrowed time into something that feels, if not permanent, at least lasting.

If the past is a memory and the present is fleeting, the future remains an enigma, a place where borrowed time extends beyond our grasp. Our relationship with the future is complex, as it holds both the promise of possibility and the fear of the unknown. Each day, we move forward, borrowing time that we cannot see, investing in a future that remains uncertain.

This UNKNOWN future shapes our choices, influencing how we live in the present. The idea that we are living on borrowed time adds weight to each decision, as we try to balance the demands of the moment with the hope of what is yet to come. In this, we experience a tension between living fully in the present and preparing for a future that may or may not arrive. It is a delicate balance, one that defines the human experience.

In the end, borrowed time is both a gift and a mystery. It offers us the chance to live, to experience, to grow, even as it reminds us that our stay here is temporary. To live on borrowed time is to accept the unknown, to embrace the beauty and fragility of each moment. It is a humbling realization, yet it can also be a source of strength, as it encourages us to live fully, to love deeply, and to find meaning in the journey.

As we move through life, aware that our time is borrowed, we learn to appreciate the small moments, to find joy in the ordinary, and to *cherish the connections we make. This awareness, far from being a burden, can become a guiding force, helping us to live with purpose and gratitude. In this, borrowed time becomes not a limitation but a profound invitation to engage with life in all its richness, to make the most of each fleeting moment.*

As we embrace borrowed time, we come to understand the paradox it presents: time is both something we are given freely, without asking, and something that, from the first moment, begins slipping through our grasp. This paradox doesn't just apply to life and death but is embedded in each day, each hour. There is always more that we want to do, more people to love, more mysteries to explore, and yet, time offers itself only in measured portions. This boundary, though often frustrating, serves as a compass that directs our priorities and refines our desires.

In the pursuit of living fully within borrowed time, we often confront the need for balance. It is easy to become caught up in pursuits of the future or regrets of the past. But time, when viewed as a borrowed gift, teaches us the profound wisdom of presence. Every moment, no matter how small or seemingly mundane, becomes significant when seen as something fleeting. The simple act of being—listening to the world around us, taking in a view, engaging in a conversation—can feel like a profound experience when we realize it may never happen in quite the same way again.

Learning to appreciate the present while still planning for the future is one of the great skills that borrowed time invites us to develop. Each decision we make, each path we choose, is influenced by the awareness that we cannot do it all. This can bring clarity, helping us focus on what matters most. Perhaps it is in this acknowledgment of limitations that we find the beauty in small things, understanding that they hold the weight of eternity within them because they are unique, unrepeatable. A single sunset, a moment of laughter, the feel of rain—each becomes irreplaceable within the brief span of time we have.

Over time, the understanding of borrowed time can cultivate a sense of acceptance. In a world that encourages relentless striving and endless ambition, there is freedom In realizing that we are not required to conquer every horizon or achieve every goal. Time humbles us, reminding us that our existence is finite. It guides us to focus on meaningful experiences and relationships, rather than just accumulation and achievement. This acceptance doesn't mean resignation but rather an appreciation of the natural ebb and flow of life. It reminds us that just as we borrow time, we also contribute to a larger tapestry that extends beyond our own individual lives.

The acceptance of borrowed time can also reshape our experience of loss. Each GOODBYE , each ending, whether expected or sudden, takes on a different significance when seen as part of a continuum. We come to realize that every relationship, every connection, is a temporary crossing of paths within the infinite movement of time. The time we share with others, no matter how brief, is meaningful precisely because it cannot last forever. This understanding deepens our appreciation of the people in our lives, knowing that each shared moment is a rare, irreplaceable intersection of time and experience.

Even though we live within the boundaries of borrowed time, there are moments that seem to defy it. Love, beauty, and creativity all hint at something beyond the temporal, offering glimpses of a timeless quality that transcends the ordinary flow of hours and days. Art, music, literature, and ideas all serve as reminders of a deeper, intangible realm. When we engage with creativity or beauty, we tap into something that seems to lie beyond time, as if borrowing not just hours but a sense of the eternal. This is why creative acts, acts of love, and moments of insight resonate so deeply—they allow us to step momentarily beyond the constraints of time.

Though these moments may be brief, they are profound, offering a sense of continuity that outlasts individual lives. It is this search for the timeless that often drives human expression, as we attempt to capture and communicate the essence of experience that is both universal and enduring. In a way, each person, in their own life, creates a narrative that adds to a collective story of humanity. This ongoing story is perhaps the closest thing to permanence we can know, a shared continuity that transcends individual lives and speaks to future generations.

The understanding of borrowed time can lead us to live with greater kindness and compassion. When we recognize that everyone around us is also living on borrowed time, our interactions take on new significance. Each encounter becomes an opportunity to connect meaningfully, to offer understanding, and to bring warmth into the lives of others. This awareness allows us to see beyond the trivial conflicts and misunderstandings that often cloud our relationships. Instead, we view each person as a fellow traveler, someone sharing in the journey of borrowed time, and this can inspire a deeper empathy and patience.

In the end, the awareness of borrowed time invites us to live with gratitude. We begin to see each moment as a gift, each experience as an opportunity, and each day as a CHANCE to engage fully with life. Gratitude shifts our perspective from scarcity to abundance, from a focus on what we lack to an appreciation of what we have. This sense of thankfulness can be transformative, allowing us to find peace within the boundaries of time rather than fighting against them.

Borrowed time, then, is not merely a limitation but a framework within which we can cultivate a meaningful life. It is the canvas on which we paint our experiences, each stroke a testament to the richness of our brief, beautiful existence. The knowledge that our time is limited is what gives life its urgency, its beauty, and its depth. It reminds us that while we cannot control the passage of time, we can choose how we spend it, who we share it with, and what we create within it.

As we continue on this journey, aware of time's finite nature, we come to see that the real gift lies not in the amount of time we have but in how we use it. Every action, every choice, and every connection becomes part of a larger whole, woven together into a unique and unrepeatable story. In this way, borrowed time is not simply something to be measured but something to be lived, cherished, and ultimately, let go of with grace.

TIME'S EMBRACE

TIME
Embracing your time
and it's moments

Time embraces all things. It flows around us, through us, carrying each life in its currents. In every moment, whether we recognize it or not, we are held in time's embrace—wrapped within its motion, its steady rhythms, its silent, invisible unfolding. Time is the vast container of existence, cradling everything, everywhere. It is an intangible force that moves without pause, pressing forward even as it nurtures the roots of all that we experience and become. Time holds us close from the first breath to the last, an invisible companion through every step of life, always present, always quietly influencing the course of our journey.

In time's embrace, everything transforms. Seeds become trees, children grow into adults, dawn turns to dusk, and then to night. Time's passage is marked by the changes it brings, and in these changes, we recognize life's progression. Nothing remains the same within time's embrace, yet there is comfort in its constancy, a reassurance that life is moving, evolving, flowing forward. We are swept along with it, held within a process that stretches from the origins of the universe to the present and beyond. Each change, each stage, is a gesture in the gentle, relentless rhythm of time.

As we grow, we learn to perceive time's embrace in subtler ways. It is there in the seasons, the cycle of birth and death, the ebb and flow of energy within nature. Time moves at different speeds for each experience; in moments of joy, it seems to fly, while in sadness, it can feel as though it lingers endlessly. This perception of time—how it stretches, compresses, pulses with intensity, or softens into stillness—shows us that time's embrace is not rigid but elastic. It adapts to the feelings it contains, shifting its texture to match the emotional weight of each experience.

Within the intimate embrace of time, we also find continuity, a connection that threads through our lives, linking the past with the present, and the present with the future. Time's embrace is like a long, winding path, each step building upon the last. Every memory we hold is a fragment of time we carry with us, like pieces of a larger puzzle that forms the picture of who we are. These memories, stitched together by time's gentle hand, create a personal history, an ongoing story that we write with every action, every choice, every word.

Time's embrace offers space for growth, allowing us to evolve, to learn, and to adapt. It cradles our successes and our failures alike, giving us the opportunity to change, to start anew, to try again. Time teaches patience by showing us that growth is gradual, that progress happens in small increments. Through time, we learn resilience, as we see how challenges are softened, their edges smoothed by the passage of days and years. Within time's embrace, we find the freedom to transform, to become who we are meant to be.

In time's embrace, we find connection to others. Each person we encounter is traveling along their own path, yet we meet, we intersect, we share moments. Time binds us together, not only with those who walk beside us but also with those who came before and those who will come after. We are part of a vast tapestry, a web of lives that intersect and influence each other. This interconnectedness gives depth to time's embrace, as it becomes not only the container for individual lives but the space in which humanity as a whole grows, learns, and evolves.

There is a certain tenderness to time's embrace. It holds the small details of everyday life: the sunlight filtering through leaves, the quiet hum of city streets at dawn, the warmth of a shared meal, the laughter of friends. These moments, though seemingly insignificant, are cradled within time, becoming part of the fabric of our days. Time preserves these memories, these impressions, and in doing so, it allows us to revisit them, to cherish them, to find meaning in them. Even the smallest moments are held within time, woven into a greater whole that shapes our understanding of life.

Time's embrace also allows us to heal. Wounds, both physical and emotional, are softened by time, as it gently layers new experiences over old pain. Time brings perspective, showing us that what once felt overwhelming is now a chapter we can look back on with acceptance. In time's embrace, we learn to forgive, to let go, to release the grip of past hurts. Time doesn't erase pain but integrates it, making it part of the larger narrative of growth and resilience. Through time, we come to see that healing is not forgetting but transforming our relationship to what has passed.

In embracing time, we come to understand the value of presence. Time moves forward, but it also offers us each present moment in its fullness, inviting us to be fully alive, fully aware, fully engaged. The present is the place where we are most alive, where we can touch time's embrace most directly. It is in the present that we experience the richness of life, the vividness of sensations, the depth of emotions. The present moment, held in time's embrace, is where life happens, where the past and future converge into a single point of experience.

Time's embrace is generous, offering us endless beginnings. Each day, each hour, is an invitation to start anew, to explore, to create. Time does not judge or discriminate; it holds every life, every story, every possibility. In time's embrace, we are free to make choices, to experiment, to learn from our mistakes. This freedom is a gift, allowing us to shape our lives according to our own desires and values. Time does not dictate what we must become; it simply offers the space in which we can become.

Yet, time's embrace is also a reminder of life's impermanence. All things must end, all experiences are finite. Time's passage brings a natural conclusion to every chapter, every relationship, every life. This awareness of impermanence can be painful, but it is also what gives life its poignancy, its beauty. Knowing that each moment is fleeting encourages us to savor it, to appreciate it, to live with a sense of urgency and gratitude. Time's embrace teaches us to hold life lightly, to cherish it without clinging, to love without the need to possess.

Ultimately, time's embrace is a source of wisdom. It teaches us to accept change, to flow with the natural rhythms of life, to trust that every experience has its season. Through time, we come to understand the cycles of beginnings and endings, growth and decay, joy and sorrow. Time teaches us that nothing is ever truly lost, that every moment, every experience, becomes part of the larger whole. It reminds us that life is a journey, not a destination, and that each step is meaningful, even if we cannot see the full pi ct ure.

In time's embrace, we find both the vastness of the universe and the intimacy of our own lives. Time connects us to everything, from the stars in the sky to the beating of our own hearts. It is the thread that weaves together all existence, binding us to a mystery that is both profound and unknowable. In surrendering to time's embrace, we discover that we are part of something greater than ourselves, something eternal, something that transcends the boundaries of individual lives.

To live in time's embrace is to live with openness, with humility, with wonder. It is to recognize that we are held within a force that is both gentle and powerful, a force that guides us, shapes us, and ultimately, releases us. Time's embrace is the silent pulse of life, the steady beat that carries us forward, reminding us that we are always part of a larger journey, always moving, always becoming. In the end, to embrace time is to embrace life itself, to find beauty in its transience, to celebrate its flow, and to trust in the unfolding mystery that it reveals.

In time's embrace, there is an acceptance of paradox: it offers us both continuity and change, permanence and impermanence, closeness and distance. To be held by time is to experience both the solidity of belonging and the lightness of letting go. Time is constant, yet it is also fleeting. This paradox invites us to understand life as a blend of holding on and releasing, a dance between memory and anticipation, between what we've known and what is yet to be discovered.

As we deepen our understanding of time's embrace, we start to recognize the richness it brings to each chapter of life. With every phase, every transformation, time wraps us in new lessons and new experiences, shaping our perception of the world. In childhood, time feels endless, a vast expanse to be explored; in youth, it accelerates, as we rush toward dreams and ambitions. In maturity, time slows, becoming more precious, each moment a reminder of life's fragility. And in age, time becomes a gentle companion, a constant presence that guides us toward reflection, memory, and peace. Time's embrace grows with us, adapting as we move through life's stages, offering the space to evolve into who we are meant to be.

Through this evolving relationship, time teaches us to value patience and perspective. In a world that often demands immediacy, time's slow, steady nature reminds us that some things cannot be rushed. Growth, healing, wisdom—all require the quiet unfolding of days, months, and years. Time's embrace holds us steady, encouraging us to move with life's natural rhythms, to allow processes to mature without force. This patience is a form of trust, an acceptance that not everything is meant to be known or achieved in a single breath.

Time's embrace also encourages us to release the fear of the unknown. The future, unseen and uncharted, can be a source of anxiety, as we yearn for certainty, for control. But in trusting time's embrace, we learn to move forward with curiosity instead of fear, to embrace uncertainty as a necessary part of life. Time shows us that the unknown is not something to be resisted but something to be explored. It becomes a place of possibility, an open canvas where we can paint new dreams, create new paths, and shape new versions of ourselves. In surrendering to time's embrace, we find freedom from the need for certainty, embracing instead the beauty of possibility.

This acceptance of the unknown brings us closer to gratitude. Each moment, held within time's embrace, becomes an opportunity to appreciate the present. Gratitude anchors us in the now, reminding us to be fully awake to the sights, sounds, and sensations around us. In time's embrace, every experience is a gift, a fleeting miracle that we are invited to hold and cherish. Gratitude allows us to see the extraordinary within the ordinary, to find wonder in the simplest of moments—a quiet morning, a familiar smile, a shared silence.

In embracing time, we learn that life is less about the destination and more about the journey. The milestones we reach, the goals we set, the successes we achieve—each is significant, but none is as important as the path itself. Time's embrace teaches us that fulfillment is found not in reaching the end but in experiencing the fullness of each step. It is in the journey that we grow, that we encounter others, that we discover who we are and who we want to become. Time invites us to savor each step, to see life as a continuous unfolding rather than a race to the finish line.

As we move forward, time's embrace reveals its quiet, profound wisdom: that we are part of a cycle far greater than ourselves. Life, in its essence, is a series of transitions, a flow of beginnings and endings. Seasons change, generations come and go, stars are born and extinguished. Time's embrace is a reminder of this larger rhythm, a gentle hum that connects us to the infinite cycles of nature and the cosmos. In accepting our place within this cycle, we find humility and connection, understanding that we are a single thread within the vast tapestry of existence.

This awareness of our place in the cycle of time deepens our sense of purpose. We come to see that every choice, every action, contributes to a legacy that extends beyond ourselves. Whether in small gestures or grand endeavors, we add to a story that is larger than our individual lives. Time's embrace offers us the opportunity to leave a mark, to create something meaningful that will resonate in the lives of others, even after we are gone. This purpose gives life depth, a sense of continuity that extends into the lives of those who come after us.

As we grow older, time's embrace takes on a new tenderness. It becomes a place of reflection, where we look back on the journey with acceptance and appreciation. Time softens the edges of memory, allowing us to see the past with clarity and compassion. In its embrace, we find the grace to forgive ourselves for the mistakes we made, to celebrate the joys we experienced, and to honor the challenges we overcame. Reflection becomes a source of peace, a way of coming to terms with our own story, understanding that every chapter—both the joyful and the difficult—was essential to our growth.

In the end, time's embrace is a reminder of life's fragility, a gentle urging to live with intention and to love without reservation. It holds us, guiding us toward a deeper understanding of ourselves and the world around us. It shows us that to live fully is to embrace each moment, to allow ourselves to be touched by beauty and to be moved by compassion, to find meaning in both the laughter and the tears. Time's embrace is a call to be present, to be open, to be fully alive.

To be held in time's embrace is to be part of something beautiful and profound, to know that we are cherished by the flow of life itself. It is a gift, an invitation to experience the richness of existence, to touch the infinite within the finite, and to understand that while our time is limited, our impact, our love, and our presence are boundless. In embracing time, we embrace life in all its fullness, and we come to see that within time's embrace, we are never truly alone.

SHADOWS OF TIME

TIME
In the shadows of time

In the shadows of time, life's mysteries and the untold stories linger, filling the spaces between moments with a silent depth. These shadows are the hidden contours of time, where memories fade, where missed chances reside, and where long-forgotten dreams sleep. Though time is often marked by the bright, visible highlights of our days—birthdays, successes, first loves—it is equally composed of these shadows, the unseen forces and forgotten events that shape us just as deeply. In the shadows of time, we confront the questions left unanswered, the lives not fully lived, and the whispers of experiences we can barely recall. It is here, in these shadows, that we find the subtle yet powerful influences that guide us quietly through life.

These shadows are woven with memories that have softened over time, becoming hazy and half-formed, slipping into the background of consciousness. Old friendships that faded away, places we once visited but rarely think about, and people who made brief yet meaningful appearances in our lives—they all linger in these shadows, held by time but just out of reach. These remnants of the past are like echoes, faint but ever-present, reminding us of who we once were, what we once valued, and how we have changed. In these quiet places, we can glimpse versions of ourselves that no longer exist, like sepia-toned portraits that reveal a more innocent or hopeful time. The shadows of time carry these memories, preserving them even as they blur, holding them as silent witnesses to our journey.

Within the shadows of time, we find the paths we did not take, the opportunities that slipped by, and the dreams that were set aside. Life is a series of choices, each one leading us down a different road, and for every decision made, there is a shadow cast by the road left unexplored. These alternate paths haunt us gently, surfacing from time to time in the form of "what if" questions, lingering curiosity, or a faint sense of nostalgia. In these shadows, there are the dreams we once held but moved away from, the ambitions we set aside in favor of practicality or obligation. Though we may try to let go of these missed possibilities, they linger quietly, serving as reminders of the infinite possibilities that time once offered us. They are the roads not taken, the alternate lives we might have lived, preserved only as shadows in the realm of time.

The shadows of time are also where we hide our regrets, the choices we wish we could undo, the words we wish we could take back. Time cannot be reversed, and so these regrets remain as silent companions, woven into our story, adding layers of complexity and depth to who we are. In the shadows, we can see these moments for what they were—mistakes, misunderstandings, missed opportunities. Over time, these regrets may soften, transforming from sharp pains into quiet reminders of our humanity, of the lessons we have learned and the growth that followed. In these shadows, time gives us perspective, allowing us to make peace with our past, to forgive ourselves, and to see the imperfections of life as essential parts of our journey.

In the shadows of time, we are reminded of loss, of the people and places that are no longer with us. Time moves forward, yet those we loved and lost remain with us, held in the quiet spaces of memory. These shadows are bittersweet, filled with traces of voices, laughter, and presence that have since faded. Though they may no longer be physically present, their essence lingers, casting long shadows that we carry within us. These shadows are both a comfort and a sorrow, reminding us of the deep connections we once had and the inevitability of change. In these moments of remembrance, time becomes a gentle custodian of our grief, holding our memories in a way that allows us to feel both the beauty of love and the ache of loss.

Time's shadows are also a place of resilience, where our struggles, challenges, and quiet victories reside. Not every triumph is celebrated openly; some of the most significant battles are fought in silence, in the privacy of our own hearts. These quiet moments of courage, the decisions we made to keep going, to heal, to rise again—they all live in the shadows, unseen but deeply felt. It is in these shadows that we recognize our strength, our ability to endure, and our capacity to grow. Time holds these moments with quiet respect, acknowledging the weight of our private journeys and the silent resilience we carry forward. In these shadows, we find a source of pride and a reminder that our strength lies not only in our visible successes but in the quiet battles that shaped us.

The shadows of time reveal to us t"e mystery of existence itself. Though we try to measure and quantify time, to divide it into hours, days, and years, it remains an enigma, an invisible force that moves us through life. In the shadows, we glimpse the limits of our understanding, the edges of what we can know and what lies beyond. Time's shadows invite us to embrace the mystery, to accept that not everything needs to be understood, that some things are meant to remain unknown. In these shadows, we find humility, a sense of awe, a quiet reverence for the vastness of time and the smallness of our own lives within it.

In the end, the shadows of time are a reminder of life's complexity, of the depth and richness of our experience. Life is not only the bright, well-lit moments; it is equally composed of these quieter, hidden spaces. The shadows of time hold our past, our dreams, our regrets, our strength, and our mysteries. They are the silent witnesses to our journey, the unseen forces that shape us in ways we may never fully understand.

To live fully is to acknowledge these shadows, to accept them as part of who we are, to recognize that they, too, have meaning and beauty. In the shadows of time, we find the parts of ourselves that are less visible but no less real—the whispers of lives unlived, the quiet strength of resilience, the grace of forgiveness, and the mystery of all that remains unknown. To walk in the shadows of time is to walk with a deeper awareness, a quieter understanding, and a profound respect for the invisible threads that connect us all.

In the shadows of time, there is a sense of timelessness, a quiet reminder that not all moments are captured by the ticking of the clock. These shadows hold our memories, regrets, and missed chances, but they also contain a strange kind of freedom. Here, outside the direct light of our schedules and routines, we are free to explore, to reflect, and to see ourselves without the labels or expectations that time often imposes on us. Time's shadows are a space where we can encounter the truest parts of ourselves, where the noise of daily life fades away, and we are left with the essence of who we are and who we wish to become.

This timeless quality also brings a sense of connection with those who came before us. The shadows of time stretch far into the past, holding the stories and struggles of countless generations. Our ancestors' dreams, fears, and triumphs echo in these spaces, linking us to a lineage that stretches back through centuries. Their lives, like ours, were marked by both light and shadow, by visible accomplishments and private challenges. In the quiet of time's shadows, we can feel this connection, sensing that we are part of something larger, a continuity that binds us across generations. Their legacies, hidden within these shadows, remind us that we are never alone in our journey, that we walk paths shaped by those who came before.

The shadows of time are also a sou"ce of wisdom, the kind that cannot be taught but only felt. This wisdom grows from the silence, from the moments spent in quiet reflection, from the acceptance of what cannot be changed. It is the understanding that life is fleeting, that pain and joy are Intertwined, and that every moment—bright or dark—has something to teach us. Time's shadows invite us to pause, to sit with our experiences, and to allow them to settle into our hearts. In doing so, we find insight, peace, and a kind of quiet strength that only comes from facing the hidden parts of life without turning away.

In these shadows, we learn the art of letting go. Not everything can be held onto forever; some dreams, relationships, and phases of life must be released. Time's shadows hold these acts of letting go, the moments when we said goodbye, when we released what no longer served us, and when we embraced the unknown. Though these moments are often painful, they are also liberating, creating space for new experiences, new relationships, and new dreams. Time's shadows remind us that endings are as much a part of life as beginnings and that by letting go, we are honoring the natural flow of time and our own need for growth.

In thc quiet corners of time's shadows, we also find forgiveness, both for others and for ourselves. Life is filled with misunderstandings, mistakes, and moments of weakness, and it is easy to carry these burdens forward. But the shadows of time offer a space for healing, a gentle reminder that we are all imperfect, all learning as we go. Here, we can reflect on our actions, accept our flaws, and find the courage to forgive. This forgiveness does not erase the past, but it transforms it, allowing us to move forward without the weight of resentment or regret. In these shadows, we find a kind of grace, an acceptance of ourselves and others that brings peace.

Ultimately, the shadows of time are where we come to terms with the mysteries of life and death. They remind us that life is not a straight line but a complex, interwoven story with many layers and dimensions. There are things we will never fully understand, questions that will remain unanswered, and endings that we cannot predict. These shadows are not something to fear but to embrace, for they are a part of life's beauty, a reminder that there is more to existence than what we can see or measure. In accepting these shadows, we learn to live with a sense of wonder, to approach life with humility, and to recognize the depth of each moment.

To walk in the shadows of time is to embrace the fullness of life—not just the bright, obvious moments but the hidden ones as well. It is to acknowledge that we are shaped as much by what we leave behind as by what we hold onto, as much by our hidden struggles as by our visible victories. These shadows teach us patience, resilience, and compassion. They remind us that there is more to each of us than meets the eye, that our lives are rich with meaning, even in the quietest, most hidden moments.

In the end, the shadows of time are a gift, a reminder that life is deeper, more complex, and more beautiful than we might realize. They hold our secrets, our silent journeys, and the wisdom we gain along the way. They are a quiet invitation to look beyond the surface, to listen to the echoes of the past, and to find peace within the mysteries of existence. In these shadows, we are reminded that life is not only about moving forward but about finding meaning in every step, about cherishing each fleeting moment, and about honoring *the journey in all its fullness.*

WAVES OF TIME

TIME
Time Waves as a wind

The waves of time, as seen through the lens of divine purpose, are more than just the rhythm of hours, days, and years. They are the ebb and flow of a greater design, a cosmic pulse that stretches beyond human understanding, embodying what many call God's time. Unlike our hurried concept of time, measured and bound by calendars and clocks, God's time is timeless, woven with an eternal patience that unfolds in the fullness of seasons. To contemplate these waves is to look beyond our limited view of moments and recognize that we are part of something vast and mysterious, a boundless tapestry that reaches beyond us and pulls us into a harmony that only God understands.

God's time does not adhere to the urgency or demands of the world. It is unhurried, a steady and measured flow that moves at its own pace. In our lives, we often desire immediacy; we want things to happen now, to see our plans fulfilled without delay. But God's time moves like the waves on a shore—persistent, cyclical, each one rolling in when it is meant to, not a moment sooner or later. These waves invite us to let go of our impatience, to trust that all things come when they are meant to. Through the waves of God's time, we are reminded to rest, to trust, and to have faith in the unfolding of life.

When we look closely at the waves of God's time, we see that every moment is part of a greater rhythm. Just as the sea has high and low tides, so too do our lives move through seasons—times of growth and times of rest, times of joy and times of sorrow. Each season has its purpose, its lessons, and its beauty, even when it is hard for us to see. What may feel like a delay, a setback, or a quiet period in our lives is often a part of God's design, a preparation for what is to come. These waves teach us to surrender our need for control and to open ourselves to the natural rhythms of life, trusting that even in stillness, God is at work.

The waves of time In God's design reveal a sense of order, a divine structure that is often hidden from our limited view. We may wonder why things happen as they do or why certain events unfold in specific ways, but within God's time, there is a purpose behind every moment. Each wave, each phase, each delay or advance is part of a larger pattern, one that we may only come to understand in hindsight or perhaps never fully grasp. This mystery is humbling, reminding us that our lives are woven into a vast and interconnected story, one that transcends our individual concerns and serves a higher purpose. In embracing this perspective, we find peace in knowing that there is meaning beyond what we can immediately see.

God's time is marked by mercy and compassion, a patience that endures across generations. It is not limited by human lifespans or historical epochs; it is eternal, stretching from the beginning of creation to the farthest reaches of eternity. In this sense, God's time is forgiving, allowing us space to grow, to learn, and to come into our own at a pace that honors our journey. We are not rushed, judged, or hurried by divine time. Instead, God's waves of time flow with a generosity that grants us room for redemption, for transformation, and for the gradual unfolding of our best selves.

When we reflect on God's time, we see that it holds a deep wisdom, a timing that knows precisely when things should come to pass. Events that seem random, delayed, or even tragic often serve a purpose that we cannot immediately understand. Like the ocean's waves that carry objects to shore in due time, God's waves bring people, experiences, and opportunities into our lives at the perfect moment. There is a sense of destiny, a feeling that everything that is meant to be will be, in the fullness of God's time. This understanding calls us to patience and to a quiet trust in the divine, knowing that all things are held within God's wisdom.

God's waves of time also carry a sense of healing. Just as water erodes, reshapes, and polishes the stones along the shore, so too do the waves of divine time heal, refine, and transform us. Old wounds, past regrets, and deep sorrows are softened, worn down over time, carried away by God's waves until only wisdom and compassion remain. This process may take years or even lifetimes, but the waves do not rush. They flow at their own pace, gently transforming us until we are ready to let go of what no longer serves us. Through God's time, we are healed, renewed, and made whole, not by our own force of will, but by surrendering to the loving rhythm of divine time.

The waves of God's time remind us of eternity, of a life that extends beyond our physical existence. Human time is fleeting, marked by beginnings and endings, arrivals and departures. But within God's time, there is no final end, only a transition into a different state of being. Just as waves return to the sea, so too do our souls return to the source from which they came. This understanding brings a sense of peace and hope, an awareness that life is not confined to this earthly experience but is part of an eternal journey, one that flows within the boundless waves of divine time.

In the end, to understand the waves of God's time is to embrace the mystery of life itself. It is to recognize that we are part of a divine design, one that moves at a pace that transcends human understanding. These waves teach us to trust, to let go, and to live with open hearts, knowing that we are held within a greater rhythm. God's time flows through us and around us, lifting us, shaping us, and guiding us toward our highest purpose. In surrendering to these waves, we find peace, knowing that we are exactly where we are meant to be, in the vast and eternal embrace of divine time.

In the unending flow of God's time, there is a serenity that invites us to rest in the knowledge that all things are progressing exactly as they should. This divine timing is a reminder that our lives, with all their triumphs and trials, are part of a sacred journey that cannot be hurried or delayed. Each experience—whether it brings joy, growth, or challenge—arrives precisely when we are ready to encounter it. In trusting these waves, we learn that even in moments of uncertainty or loss, we are not adrift; we are being guided by a hand that sees the greater picture, one that lovingly shapes each season of our lives with purpose.

These waves carry a wisdom that whispers to us, asking us to slow down and listen, to feel the divine presence that flows quietly through every day. In the rush of our schedules, it's easy to overlook the gentle nudges and subtle signs that come to us through God's timing. But the waves of divine time are patient, calling us to a slower rhythm, one that honors the depth and beauty of each moment. In aligning ourselves with this rhythm, we begin to see life differently—not as a series of isolated events, but as an interconnected tapestry woven with love, purpose, and grace.

In the gentle sway of God's time, we find that life is not solely about arriving at specific milestones or achieving certain goals. Instead, it is about the journey itself, about being fully present in each step, trusting that we are always being led toward what is meant for us. The waves of divine time call us to release our attachments to specific outcomes and to embrace the idea that there is beauty in simply being, in allowing life to unfold as it will. By doing so, we open ourselves to unexpected blessings, to the hidden gifts that arrive when we are least expecting them but most in need.

God's waves of time also teach us the sacred art of waiting. Waiting is often uncomfortable, a space where we feel vulnerable or uncertain. But in divine time, waiting is not an empty pause; it is a time of preparation, a quiet nurturing of the soul. Just as seeds are buried in the dark soil before they sprout, we too undergo silent growth during seasons of waiting. These times of pause are woven with purpose, refining us, strengthening our patience, and deepening our faith. The waves remind us that waiting is not a passive state, but a sacred space where we gather strength and wisdom for what lies ahead.

As the waves of divine time flow through us, we begin to see that we are part of something far greater than ourselves. Our lives, our struggles, and our dreams are all pieces of a much larger story—a story that God is crafting with infinite care. Each person, each moment, and each experience we encounter is connected, woven together by the timeless love that flows through all things. This perspective brings a profound sense of belonging, a realization that we are not isolated or insignificant, but rather essential threads in the vast fabric of existence. It reminds us that our lives, however small they may seem, contribute to the beauty and harmony of the world.

In God's time, there is no hurry, no rush to achieve or to prove. Instead, there is a quiet assurance that everything is unfolding as it should. This divine patience invites us to release the pressures and anxieties we carry, to let go of the feeling that we must constantly push forward. God's waves remind us that our worth is not measured by our accomplishments, but by the love we bring to each moment, the kindness we extend to others, and the peace we find within ourselves. In embracing this perspective, we begin to live in a state of grace, moving through life with a sense of calm and purpose that transcends worldly expectations.

The waves of divine time also reveal to us the power of transformation. Just as the tides reshape the shoreline over time, God's time gently reshapes us, molding us into who we are meant to become. This transformation is often subtle, occurring gradually over years, through experiences both joyful and painful. We may not always see the changes as they happen, but as we look back, we realize that each wave, each season, has brought us closer to our true selves. In divine time, there is always space for growth, for healing, and for the emergence of new beginnings.

In God's time, there is also an invitation to experience deep gratitude. When we see life through the lens of divine timing, we recognize the abundance that surrounds us—the small miracles, the gentle guidance, the moments of peace that flow into our lives unexpectedly. These waves remind us to pause, to savor the beauty of the present moment, to give thanks for the countless blessings that fill our days. Gratitude becomes a way of aligning ourselves with the rhythm of divine time, a way of saying "yes" to the life that is unfolding before us, with all its mystery and wonder.

As we learn to trust the waves of God's time, we find that even the uncertainties of life take on a new meaning. We realize that we don't need to have all the answers or to see the full path ahead; we only need to trust in the next step, to have faith that we are being guided toward what is best for us. This trust allows us to release our fears, to walk forward with a sense of hope and assurance that we are held within God's love. In this trust, we find a peace that surpasses understanding, a quiet knowing that we are exactly where we are meant to be.

To live in harmony with God's waves of time is to live with an open heart, ready to embrace each moment, each lesson, and each blessing as it arrives. It is to let go of our attachment to timelines and plans, and to surrender to a greater wisdom, a divine rhythm that knows our hearts, our desires, and our purpose. It is to live with a sense of awe and wonder, knowing that each wave carries us closer to the fulfillment of who we are meant to be, held within the boundless love and grace of God's eternal time.

In the end, the waves of God's time are a gift, an invitation to trust in the journey, to find beauty in the mystery, and to rest in the assurance that we are always being carried forward. These waves remind us that we are never alone, that we are always moving within a divine flow that holds us, guides us, and leads us to our truest self. To live within these waves is to live with a peace that comes from knowing we are deeply loved, part of a greater story that unfolds with perfect timing, and embraced by the eternal presence of God's time.

As we rest in the rhythm of God's time, we come to realize that each moment, each wave, holds within it a sacred calling—to be fully present, to engage with life as it is given, and to trust that every experience holds meaning. The waves of divine time remind us that nothing is wasted; each joy and sorrow, each success and struggle, each connection and departure is woven into our lives with purpose. In embracing this, we are freed from the need to rush through or control our path, and instead, we are encouraged to live with intention and openness, knowing that we are continually being shaped for something greater.

These waves carry within them the essence of divine love—a love that is patient, kind, and unconditional. God's time is not simply about progression or change; it is about the growth of the soul, the flowering of our deepest potential. In every wave that rolls forward, we are invited to let go of old fears, to release what no longer serves us, and to move closer to the core of who we truly are. Divine time is a constant reminder that love is at the center of everything, that the pulse of God's waves is the very heartbeat of creation, calling us back to ourselves and to one another.

Through this lens, we come to understand that God's time does not separate us from each other, but rather draws us closer, uniting us in a shared journey that spans generations, cultures, and even lifetimes. The waves of divine time wash over us all, binding us in a collective story of human experience, each of us a part of a larger whole. When we live with this awareness, we feel a profound kinship with others, a recognition that we are all being carried by the same waves, guided by the same divine hand. This understanding cultivates within us a sense of compassion, empathy, and unity, reminding us that our lives are not isolated but interconnected.

In the quiet moments when we feel these waves most clearly, we are often drawn to prayer, reflection, or meditation, those sacred practices that allow us to align ourselves with God's timing. In these moments, we let go of the noise and distractions of the world, allowing ourselves to be still, to listen, and to feel the gentle rhythm of divine time moving within us. This practice brings us closer to a sense of peace and grounding, a reminder that even when life feels chaotic, the waves of God's time are steady and unchanging, guiding us back to the center.

Divine time teaches us to approach life with humility. It reminds us that we are not the sole architects of our destiny, that there is a wisdom far greater than our own at work in our lives. When we surrender our need to control every detail, we allow God's time to lead us in ways that we could never have planned. This surrender is not a loss of power, but rather an embrace of freedom, a release from the burdens of worry and doubt. It is in this letting go that we find our truest power, for we are then moving with the flow of divine time, allowing ourselves to be shaped by a force that knows us deeply and loves us fully.

In the waves of God's time, there is also a profound invitation to creativity and growth. Just as the tides continually reshape the shoreline, divine time encourages us to evolve, to create, and to bring forth beauty in all that we do. Each season of our lives offers new opportunities to learn, to express, and to contribute. When we align with these waves, we feel inspired to engage with life in a way that is genuine and fulfilling, trusting that our unique gifts and talents are part of God's purpose. Divine time calls us to live with passion and authenticity, to create and to share our light with the world.

Ultimately, the waves of God's time teach us about the sacredness of all things, the holiness present in every breath, every step, every connection we make. Divine time is not just something that moves around us; it is something that flows through us, filling each moment with the possibility of grace. As we open ourselves to these waves, we find that life is not divided into sacred and ordinary, but that all of it is sacred. Every encounter, every experience, every wave of time carries the potential for transformation, for healing, for love.

In God's time, we discover that there is nothing to fear. The unknown, the uncertain, and the unseen all find their place within this divine flow. The waves of God's time carry us, gently but surely, toward our truest purpose, toward a life that reflects the love and wisdom of the

Creator. And in embracing these waves, we come to trust not only in God's timing but in our own journey, knowing that each wave brings us closer to the fulfillment of our soul's path.

So we rest in this divine rhythm, knowing that we are loved, that we are held, and that we are part of something vast and beautiful. We let the waves of God's time carry us forward, one breath, one moment, one wave at a time, trusting that we are exactly where we are meant to be, and that all things are unfolding in perfect harmony. In this embrace of divine time, we find peace, purpose, and a joy that transcends all understanding—a joy rooted in the knowledge that we are always, always carried by the waves of God's eternal love

MOMENTS LOST TO TIME

TIME
Loosing great
moments to time

Moments lost to time slip through our grasp, fading like whispers on the wind, carried beyond our reach. These moments, whether fleeting instances of joy, connection, or even regret, belong now to the past. Time, with its relentless pace, collects each experience and tucks it away into memory. There is a bittersweet quality to these lost moments—part of us yearns to hold onto them, to keep them vivid and present, yet they are the very definition of impermanence. They are reminders of the nature of life itself, constantly changing, continually moving forward, leaving only memories in its wake.

The advantages of moments lost to time are often hidden but can reveal profound truths. These moments help us live more intentionally, as the awareness that time is fleeting encourages us to cherish each experience. Knowing that every second is temporary can inspire us to be fully present, to savor each encounter, each conversation, each sunrise. This awareness brings a deeper appreciation for life's small joys, the warmth of a friend's laughter, the beauty of a quiet afternoon. When we accept that these moments will pass, we learn to value them more deeply and to live without taking our time for granted.

Another advantage of moments lost to time is that they allow us to grow. Experiences that were once sharp or painful eventually soften and become a part of our past, allowing us to move forward. Time acts as a natural healer, taking the rawness of difficult moments and transforming them into lessons or even wisdom. By letting go of the past, we open space for the future. This process of loss and letting go is essential for personal growth; it allows us to evolve, to make new choices, and to approach life with fresh perspectives unburdened by the weight of past moments. The passing of time can help us forgive, let go of regret, and find peace in ways that we couldn't have achieved if we clung too tightly to what has been.

Moments lost to time also grant us freedom. By letting moments pass, we are not defined solely by any single experience but by the tapestry of all our experiences combined. This freedom lets us reinvent ourselves, to continue shaping who we are without being anchored by a past version of ourselves. The impermanence of time allows us to constantly change, to adapt, and to build upon our lives in new ways. Each moment that fades gives us permission to start anew, to keep growing, to make different choices that better reflect who we are becoming.

However, the passing of time also has its disadvantages, especially when it comes to the loss of treasured moments. The most precious memories—whether of loved ones, achievements, or beautiful experiences—can begin to fade, leaving us with only fragments of what once felt so vivid. This gradual loss can bring a sense of nostalgia, a longing for something that was once real but is now beyond our reach. These moments, though gone, often carry pieces of our heart with them. We may find ourselves wishing we could return to them, that we could hold onto the feelings, the connections, the sense of wholeness they once gave us. This desire to grasp at time, to preserve what we once cherished, is a natural response to the reality of loss and change.

Another disadvantage of moments lost to time is that, as memories fade, details become blurred, and we may begin to lose sight of certain aspects of ourselves and our history. Events that shaped us, decisions that once felt monumental, and experiences that taught us crucial lessons can recede into the background, making it harder to recall the full scope of who we are and where we came from. These lost details may make us feel disconnected from our past, as if parts of ourselves have drifted away. This can create a sense of disorientation, a feeling that we are not fully rooted in our own story.

Moments lost to time can also bring about a sense of regret. We may look back and wish we had acted differently, said something we left unspoken, or seized an opportunity that we let pass by. These missed chances can linger in our minds, creating a subtle ache or feeling of incompleteness. Time's passage can feel like a barrier that prevents us from revisiting or correcting these moments, leaving us with a sense of what could have been. In this way, lost moments become a reminder of life's fragility and our own limitations—a reminder that once a moment is gone, it cannot be reclaimed.

And yet, these disadvantages are not without purpose. They are invitations to live more consciously, to recognize the fleeting nature of time and to respond with intention and awareness. When we feel the weight of lost moments, we are reminded to fully embrace the present. The ache of regret, the sorrow of fading memories, these are calls to action—an encouragement to live with fewer regrets, to speak our truth, to savor each day with an open heart. They invite us to be intentional, to make choices that align with our truest values, and to love deeply while we have the chance.

In this balance between advantage and disadvantage lies the true essence ~~*of life. Moments lost to time teach us about both the richness and the fragility of existence. They remind us that life is not meant to be clung to but lived fully and freely, embracing each moment while allowing it to pass when the time comes. The beauty of life lies in its transience, in the knowledge that every moment is a gift that will soon become a memory. This understanding calls us to live with gratitude, to cherish what we have while we have it, and to release it when it is time.*~~

Ultimately, moments lost to time shape us in profound ways. They deepen our empathy, our understanding, and our connection to others. They teach us to live with open hearts, to value each fleeting encounter, and to find peace in the knowledge that, while moments may pass, the impact of our experiences, our love, and our choices continues. Though time moves forward, what we have lived remains within us, not as something we can hold onto, but as something that has shaped who we are. In this, we find a sense of continuity, a reminder that while moments may be lost to time, their essence remains, carried within us as we move forward, forever influenced by all that has been.

As we reflect on moments lost to time, we begin to understand that their impermanence doesn't diminish their significance; in fact, it enhances it. Each moment, as it passes, becomes part of an invisible mosaic that forms the entirety of who we are. These moments are gone from the present, yet they live on in us, shaping our perspectives, guiding our choices, and influencing our actions. In this way, time becomes a quiet sculptor, chipping away at what no longer serves us while polishing and refining the aspects that define our growth. Each lost moment, whether joyful, painful, or mundane, is a thread that has been woven into our internal fabric.

Living in the awareness of moments lost to time also invites us to cultivate mindfulness. When we realize that each experience is fleeting, we are inspired to engage with life more fully. Simple, everyday occurrences—a conversation with a loved one, the feel of sunlight, the smell of fresh rain—take on a richness they might otherwise lack. This awareness brings us into the present, reminding us that now is the only moment we truly possess. When we embrace this mindset, we transform routine into reverence, giving value to things that might otherwise go unnoticed. In this way, our days become filled with meaning, with a sense of beauty and depth that transcends the ordinary.

Moments lost to time also highlight the wisdom in embracing change. Just as the seasons shift, so too do the chapters of our lives. We are not the same as we were a year ago, a week ago, or even a day ago. This constant evolution is a gift, allowing us to continually redefine and refine ourselves. Time teaches us to let go, to release our grip on what was, and to allow ourselves to grow in new directions. When we resist this natural flow, we create unnecessary suffering, holding onto memories or past versions of ourselves that no longer align with who we are becoming. But when we surrender to the rhythm of change, we find freedom, realizing that every ending is also a beginning, that every loss makes room for something new.

There is also a certain liberation in knowing that time carries everything forward, beyond our control. We are relieved of the need to keep everything alive and present, as if each memory or experience were something to be preserved indefinitely. Instead, we can appreciate the beauty of transience, recognizing that it is not our role to cling to every moment, but rather to let each one pass through us, to live it fully and then let it go. This surrender allows us to release the weight of expectation, to stop trying to capture or perfect every aspect of our lives, and to accept the flow as it is, imperfect and impermanent.

Moments lost to time also teach us about resilience. Every person faces struggles, losses, and challenges, and each of these moments fades into the past, often leaving behind strength and wisdom. The heartache that once felt overwhelming eventually becomes a memory, softened by time and transmuted into resilience. This is the quiet gift of time: it takes the sharp edges of our sorrows and smooths them over, helping us to heal, grow, and move forward. Though we may still carry echoes of pain, we also gain a sense of perspective, a recognition that we have weathered storms and emerged stronger. We learn to trust in our own ability to endure, to find light even when moments feel dark.

Yet, there is also a quiet sadness that accompanies the awareness of moments lost to time. We feel the absence of what has passed, the people and places that have slipped away, and the innocence or optimism of younger days. This awareness brings with it a sense of nostalgia, a yearning for something that can never be reclaimed. However, within this sadness lies a beautiful lesson: that our love, our care, and our memories are powerful because they are fleeting. The sadness we feel is a reflection of the depth of our connection, the importance we assign to what we have experienced. It is a gentle reminder that, while we cannot hold onto everything, the love and meaning we attach to our moments give them an enduring value that time cannot erase.

In the end, the advantages and disadvantages of moments lost to time are two sides of the same coin. Our awareness of impermanence gives life meaning, reminding us to embrace each experience, to savor what we have while we have it, and to release it when it's time. It is through this balance—between cherishing and letting go—that we come to understand the true richness of life. The beauty of our existence lies not in permanence but in the fleetingness of each experience, each encounter, each day. Time, by taking each moment away, encourages us to live fully, to love deeply, and to face each day with a heart open to whatever it brings.

Perhaps the most profound gift of moments lost to time is the realization that while we cannot hold onto every experience, the essence of what we have lived remains. Each memory, each feeling, each choice leaves an imprint on us, becoming part of the larger story of who we are. Our lives may be brief, but they are rich with meaning, layered with countless moments that, though lost to time, contribute to the depth and complexity of our soul. And so, we continue forward, with the understanding that while time will take each moment away, the love, wisdom, and growth we have gained remain with us, shaping us and guiding us as we walk through the ever-unfolding journey of life.

SUBTANCE OF TIME

TIME
What's this time as a substance

Time is a substance we cannot touch, yet it shapes all that we know. It is an invisible thread woven through every life, every moment, every memory. Time has no physical form, no weight or color, yet it is as real and as present as anything in existence. It surrounds us, moves through us, and though it is beyond our control, it accompanies every step of our journey. Time is a substance of experience and transformation, marking the boundaries of existence and giving meaning to the moments within.

Time, in its essence, is a paradox. It is both vast and fleeting, both constant and mutable. To some, time feels linear, a straight path from the past through the present and into the future. But to others, time is cyclical, a series of endless rotations, with each moment leading seamlessly into the next. And for others still, time feels like a fluid substance, flowing and ebbing, expanding and contracting depending on the experience at hand. Time shifts, changes, morphs according to our perception, our emotions, our memories. It can feel slow in moments of sorrow or pain, stretching each second into an eternity, or it can fly by in a flash of joy and connection, leaving us breathless in its wake.

The substance of time is elusive. It cannot be seen or held, yet it can be felt profoundly. Time is both a backdrop and an active force, both a setting and a character in our lives. It shapes the contours of our days, gives rhythm to our routines, and holds the weight of our histories. Time gives structure to our lives, grounding us in a shared reality where we can meet others, share experiences, create memories. Time is the stage upon which life unfolds, a canvas that allows for growth, transformation, and change.

Within time, there is space for memory and anticipation. Memory is our way of capturing and preserving moments that have passed, giving us a sense of continuity and identity. Anticipation, on the other hand, is our way of reaching into the future, of dreaming and planning for what is yet to come. These two forces—memory and anticipation—are both reflections of time's substance. Memory anchors us, connecting us to the past and to our own story, while anticipation pulls us forward, filling us with hope, with fear, with dreams. Together, they form the boundaries of our existence within time, allowing us to navigate the present while carrying the weight of the past and the promise of the future.

Time, as a substance, is intimately tied to change. It is the agent of transformation, the force that carries us from one state to another. Every living thing, every object, every atom in the universe is subject to time's influence. Time shapes us from birth to death, from innocence to wisdom, from hope to understanding. It is time that allows for growth, for learning, for healing. Without time, nothing would progress, nothing would evolve, nothing would come to fruition. Time is the catalyst for all change, the silent force that turns seeds into trees, children into adults, and dreams into reality.

The substance of time Is interwoven with cycles—days and nights, seasons, life and death. Each cycle is a reminder of time's presence, of its continuous movement. The sun rises and sets, the moon waxes and wanes, the earth tilts and spins, and life goes on. These cycles give time a sense of rhythm, a heartbeat that pulses through nature and through our lives. In understanding these cycles, we gain a deeper appreciation for the passage of time, for the beauty of beginnings and endings, for the intricate dance between birth and decay. Time's cycles are a testament to its enduring nature, a reminder that even as moments pass, time itself remains.

The substance of time Is felt most deeply in moments of transition. There are times in life when we stand on the threshold of change, poised between what was and what will be. These are moments of intensity, of heightened awareness, as we feel the weight of time pressing upon us. In these moments, time seems to slow, to expand, to make room for reflection and understanding. It is in these spaces—between the past and the future—that we feel the true substance of time, as it holds us, supports us, and guides us through the process of transformation.

Time is also the substance of impermanence. It teaches us that nothing lasts forever, that all things are transient, that life is a series of fleeting moments. This impermanence can be difficult to accept, as it reminds us of our own mortality, of the fragility of everything we hold dear. But within this impermanence, there is also beauty. Time's transience gives value to each moment, each relationship, each experience. It reminds us to cherish what we have, to live fully, to appreciate the present. Time's impermanence is both a gift and a challenge, urging us to find meaning in the here and now.

Though we experience time individually, it is a substance that connects us all. Every person, every living being, exists within time, sharing in the same cycles, the same moments, the same progression. This shared experience creates a sense of unity, a bond that transcends cultures, languages, and beliefs. Time is the common ground upon which we all stand, the universal measure by which we all live. It is a reminder that we are all part of a larger whole, that we are all moving through life together, each of us carrying our own stories, our own struggles, our own joys, but all united by the steady march of time.

The substance of time also contains echoes of eternity. Though time is measured, divided, categorized, it also hints at something beyond, something infinite. There are moments when time seems to dissolve, when we feel a sense of timelessness, a connection to something eternal. These moments may come in the presence of beauty, in deep meditation, in love, or in the quiet stillness of nature. In these rare, profound experiences, we sense that time is not just a linear progression but a doorway to something greater. Time is both finite and infinite, both a path and a destination, both a means and an end.

In contemplating the substance of time, we are reminded of our own role within it. Time gives us the opportunity to create, to contribute, to make a difference. It is within the substance of time that we leave our mark, whether through art, ideas, relationships, or acts of kindness. Our actions, though fleeting, are woven into the fabric of time, becoming part of a legacy that endures beyond our individual lives. Time allows us to shape the world, to touch the lives of others, to build a future that reflects our values, our dreams, our hopes. In this way, time is both a gift and a responsibility, an invitation to live with purpose and to create meaning.

Ultimately, the substance of time is mystery. It is something we experience but cannot fully understand, something we measure but cannot contain. Time is both ordinary and extraordinary, both familiar and unknowable. It holds the secrets of the universe, the mysteries of existence, the answers to questions we have yet to ask. In embracing the mystery of time, we find peace in the unknown, in the realization that some things are meant to be felt rather than understood.

Time is the substance that binds us, shapes us, teaches us, and ultimately, frees us. It is the silent witness to every joy, every sorrow, every triumph, and every loss. In understanding time, we come to understand life itself, to see that every moment, every heartbeat, is a precious part of a larger whole. Time is not just a measure but a medium, not just a force but a companion. It is the invisible thread that weaves our stories together, the silent river that carries us forward, the substance in which we find ourselves, our purpose, and our place in the universe.

To live within the substance of time is to live with awareness, with gratitude, with wonder. It is to embrace the fullness of life, to honor the past, to embrace the present, and to step into the future with open arms. Time is a substance that flows through all things, binding us to each other, to the world, and to something infinitely larger. It is the essence of existence, the heartbeat of life, the silent echo of eternity. In the end, the substance of time is both the journey and the destination, the means and the meaning, the mystery and the miracle that holds us all.

Time affects us in ways both profound and subtle, shaping who we are, how we think, and how we experience the world. It is woven into every part of our lives, from our physical bodies to our memories, emotions, and sense of self. Time doesn't just pass around us; it leaves its imprint on us, molding our perspectives and influencing the choices we make. Though we may not always notice its presence, time is an invisible force that shapes our reality, defining our growth, our relationships, our ambitions, and our deepest understanding of existence.

One of the most visible effects of time is on our physical bodies. Every cell, every heartbeat, every breath is marked by time's steady progression. We grow, we age, and we change, all according to time's natural rhythm. Our bodies are like instruments that tune themselves to the passage of time, adapting to the cycles of days, months, and years. This physical impact of time reminds us of our own mortality, of the inevitable nature of aging. It brings an awareness that life is limited, that every day we are a step further along the journey, encouraging us to value our health and take care of our bodies as best we can.

Time also has a profound effect on our emotions and memories. Moments that are joyous, sorrowful, or intense seem to linger in our minds, while other periods of time may blur together or fade entirely. Time gives our memories structure and context, allowing us to revisit the past and carry forward the lessons we have learned. As time passes, painful experiences can soften, and our perspective may change. Time allows us to heal from grief, to forgive, to gain wisdom. In this way, time becomes a source of emotional growth, helping us to understand, accept, and integrate our experiences.

Our perception of time also shapes our choices, values, and priorities. When we are young, time feels abundant, stretching out endlessly before us. We may feel a sense of invincibility, a belief that there will always be more time to do the things we want. But as we grow older, we begin to feel time's limitations more acutely. This awareness can bring clarity, encouraging us to focus on what truly matters, to let go of superficial concerns, and to invest our energy in the relationships, goals, and pursuits that bring us fulfillment. Time acts as a filter, allowing us to refine our lives according to our most important values.

In relationships, time has a unique and profound effect. It is the foundation upon which bonds are built, allowing trust, love, and intimacy to grow. The time we share with others—whether moments or years—deepens our connections, creating memories and shared experiences that bring us closer together. Time allows relationships to evolve, to mature, and to adapt to new circumstances. It also teaches us about letting go, as people come and go, and we must learn to cherish the time we had with them without clinging to what is no longer present. In this way, time shapes our understanding of love, teaching us to appreciate each moment and to hold others with compassion and grace.

Our ambitions and achievements are also shaped by time. The goals we set, the dreams we pursue, the efforts we make—all are influenced by our sense of time. Deadlines, milestones, and life stages create a structure for our aspirations, giving us a timeline against which we measure our progress. Time provides the motivation to work hard, to push forward, to strive for success, as we know that opportunities may be limited. It gives urgency to our ambitions, a sense of purpose that drives us to create, to innovate, to contribute. At the same time, time teaches us patience, showing us that meaningful accomplishments often require sustained effort, perseverance, and resilience.

Time influences our perception of the world and the meaning we derive from life. Knowing that time is finite makes life more precious, urging us to appreciate each moment and to live with a sense of purpose. The understanding that time is constantly moving forward encourages us to embrace change, to let go of regrets, and to focus on the present. Time's passage reminds us that life is a journey, a continuous unfolding, where each stage has its unique joys and challenges. This perspective helps us to find meaning in both the highs and lows, to see life not as a collection of isolated moments but as a coherent, evolving story.

One of the deepest effects of time is the perspective it brings. With time, we gain a greater understanding of ourselves, of others, and of the world. What once seemed critical or insurmountable often becomes manageable or even insignificant with the passage of time. Time allows us to step back, to see the bigger picture, and to develop a broader perspective that encompasses more than our immediate concerns. This shift in perspective can bring a sense of peace, as we come to understand that life's challenges are part of a larger process of growth and discovery.

Time also teaches us resilience. Life is filled with difficulties, losses, and unexpected turns, and time is what carries us through these moments. It shows us that pain is temporary, that sorrow will fade, that hope can return. Time gives us the strength to keep going, to endure, and to trust that even the darkest days will pass. This resilience, born of time's passage, becomes a source of inner strength, helping us to face future challenges with courage and grace.

In the end, time affects us by making us more fully human. It shapes our memories, our growth, our relationships, our ambitions, our perspectives. It teaches us humility, as we come to understand that we are part of something much larger than ourselves. It teaches us gratitude, as we learn to appreciate the fleeting beauty of each moment. It teaches us compassion, as we recognize that everyone is walking their own path through time, facing their own joys and struggles. And it teaches us acceptance, as we come to terms with life's impermanence, with the knowledge that everything, including ourselves, is part of an ongoing, ever-changing flow.

Ultimately, time affects us by reminding us of our own humanity—our fragility, our resilience, our capacity for love, and our drive for meaning.

Time is the silent force that shapes our journey, guiding us through life's transitions, encouraging us to grow, to learn, and to become the fullest expression of ourselves. To be affected by time is to be deeply, beautifully alive, to experience the full spectrum of existence, and to know that within the boundaries of time, we have the opportunity to live, to love, and to leave a legacy that endures beyond our years.

GOD'S TIME

TIME
An ordained Time
For you

In the unfolding of our da

fabric of our lives, inviting us to step back, breathe, and embrace the rhythm of His divine purpose.

Every moment of our lives is marked by His presence, and each experience is a thread in the greater tapestry of our existence. In God's time, moments are not merely fleeting; they hold the potential for transformation, revelation, and connection. It is essential to understand that while we operate in a world governed by time, we can align ourselves with the divine timing that shapes our journeys.

God's time teaches us patience. In a society that values speed and efficiency, waiting can feel burdensome. Yet, waiting in faith allows us to cultivate trust. Just as a seed must be buried in darkness before it can sprout, so too must we often endure seasons of waiting to witness the blossoming of God's promises. This period of waiting can be a powerful opportunity for growth, reflection, and preparation for what lies ahead.

In our lives, we may encounter moments of uncertainty or detours that seem frustrating. However, these are not mere interruptions but divine appointments. God's timing may lead us to unexpected places, relationships, and opportunities. When we surrender our timelines to Him, we open ourselves to the blessings and lessons that arise from His perfect plan.

Recognizing God's time also invites us to be present in the moment. Each day is a gift, filled with opportunities to encounter His love and grace. By practicing mindfulness, we can appreciate the beauty of the ordinary—the laughter of a friend, the warmth of the sun, the quiet moments of solitude. In these small instances, we can see the fingerprints of God's timing in our lives, reminding us that He is intimately involved in every detail.

Our understanding of time often emphasizes what is next—what we have to accomplish, who we need to meet, where we need to be. Yet, in God's time, the focus shifts from what lies ahead to what is happening now. Each day carries the potential for divine encounters, lessons learned, and grace received. It calls us to trust that we are exactly where we need to be, even when we cannot see the bigger picture.

God's time also encourages us to reflect on our priorities. What truly matters? In the hustle of daily life, we can easily lose sight of our purpose. God's timing prompts us to align our actions with our values, reminding us to invest in relationships, pursue our passions, and serve others. As we embrace His time, we cultivate a life that reflects His love and purpose, allowing our actions to become a testimony of His goodness.

Through prayer, we can deepen our understanding of God's time. In moments of stillness, we can seek His guidance, aligning our hearts with His will. Prayer becomes a sacred conversation where we surrender our anxieties about the future and trust in His perfect timing. It is in these moments of intimacy that we gain clarity, strength, and peace, knowing that our lives are held in the hands of the One who knows the end from the beginning.

As we journey through life, we will encounter seasons of change—some joyful, some challenging. In these moments, it is essential to remember that

God's time remains constant. He walks alongside us, guiding us through transitions, providing comfort in grief, and celebrating our victories. Each season serves a purpose in our spiritual growth, shaping us into the individuals He has created us to be.

In conclusion, embracing God's time for our lives means recognizing that we are part of a larger narrative, a story written by the Author of time itself. It invites us to release our anxieties, trust in His plan, and engage fully in the present moment. By doing so, we can experience the richness of life as we align ourselves with His divine timing, finding purpose and peace in every season.

In the tapestry of our lives, may we learn to weave the threads of God's time into our everyday existence, discovering that His timing is always perfect, and His love is always present.

As we delve deeper into the understanding of God's time in our lives, we begin to see that it is not merely a passive acceptance of circumstances but an active engagement with His divine purpose. We are invited to participate in a rhythm that transcends the chaos around us, moving in harmony with the Creator's heartbeat. This engagement begins with cultivating an awareness of God's presence in our daily lives.

Cultivating Awareness

Awareness is the foundation of experiencing God's time. In the busyness of our routines, we can often miss the subtle ways He is working. To cultivate this awareness, we can practice gratitude—acknowledging the gifts, big and small, that fill our days. By keeping a gratitude journal or taking moments to reflect on what we are thankful for, we train our hearts to recognize the divine fingerprints all around us. Each note of gratitude becomes a reminder that God's timing is active and that He is continuously providing for our needs.

Another practice is the discipline of silence and solitude. In a world filled with noise, finding moments of stillness allows us to reconnect with God's presence. Whether through meditation, prayer, or simply sitting in nature, these moments become sacred spaces where we can hear His voice more clearly. In these quiet times, we can lay our burdens before Him, seeking clarity and direction.

Trusting the Process

As we cultivate awareness, we are also called to trust the process. God's time often requires us to let go of our timelines and embrace uncertainty. Trusting in God's plan means believing that He is working even when we cannot see the outcome. It is an act of faith that challenges us to release control and surrender to His wisdom.

This trust can be especially difficult during seasons of waiting or struggle. We may question why things aren't happening as we desire or why we face challenges that seem insurmountable. In these moments, we can find comfort in Scripture. Verses like Jeremiah 29:11 remind us that God has plans for our lives—plans to prosper us and not to harm us, plans to give us hope and a future. When we lean on His promises, we can face uncertainty with confidence.

Embracing Seasons of Change

Life is marked by seasons—each with its own beauty and challenges. Understanding God's time helps us navigate these seasons with grace. In spring, we may experience new beginnings, fresh opportunities, and growth. In summer, we enjoy the fruits of our labor, basking in joy and abundance. In autumn, we may face transitions and let go of what no longer serves us, making room for new growth. In winter, we may experience stillness, reflection, and preparation for what is to come.

Each season is essential to our spiritual journey. Just as nature goes through cycles, so do our lives. Embracing these seasons allows us to appreciate the ebb and flow of our experiences, recognizing that God is present in each phase. When we acknowledge the uniqueness of our current season, we can find purpose in the process, knowing that each moment contributes to our growth and transformation.

Building Community

As we journey through life, we are not meant to walk alone. Building a supportive community is vital to understanding God's timing in our lives. Surrounding ourselves with individuals who share our faith can encourage us to trust in God's plan. In community, we find strength, accountability, and encouragement. Sharing our stories and experiences can illuminate how God is working in our lives and inspire others to recognize His timing in their own.

Engaging in fellowship through small groups, church activities, or service projects allows us to connect with others and experience God's love in action. These relationships remind us that we are part of a larger body, each member playing a unique role in God's design. In community, we can celebrate victories, support one another in struggles, and learn from each other's journeys.

Living in Purpose

Ultimately, understanding God's time calls us to live with intention and purpose. When we align our lives with His timing, we begin to see our everyday actions as opportunities to reflect His love and grace. This alignment invites us to serve others, pursue our passions, and share our unique gifts with the world.

Our purpose is often revealed in the small, seemingly mundane moments of life. A smile shared with a stranger, a helping hand offered to a neighbor, or a listening ear for a friend—all these actions are reflections of God's love in motion. By living intentionally, we become vessels of His grace, allowing His light to shine through us in a world that desperately needs hope and compassion.

As we conclude this exploration of God's time for our lives, we are reminded that this journey is ongoing. Embracing God's time is not a one-time decision but a daily commitment to trust, reflect, and engage with the world around us.

Let us approach each day with a heart open to His leading, seeking to recognize the sacred in the ordinary. In moments of waiting, let us find peace in His presence. In seasons of change, let us trust in His purpose. In the midst of busyness, let us cultivate awareness of the beauty that surrounds us.

May we strive to live fully in the present, knowing that every moment is a gift from God. As we align our lives with His divine timing, we can navigate the complexities of life with grace, finding joy in the journey and purpose in each step. Ultimately, God's time is an invitation to live abundantly, to love deeply, and to walk faithfully in the light of His presence.

EPILOGUE

Moments Lost to Time concludes with a gentle reminder of life's impermanence and the beauty held within each passing moment. While we cannot preserve every experience or hold onto each cherished memory, we carry forward their essence, woven into the fabric of who we are. This book invites readers to embrace both the sweetness and sorrow of time's passage, recognizing that true meaning lies not in permanence but in fully living and appreciating each moment as it comes. As we part with these reflections, Moments Lost to Time leaves us with a sense of quiet peace and renewed purpose. It encourages us to live with openness, to honor the lessons of the past, and to step forward with gratitude and grace. In accepting the transience of life, we find not loss, but a deeper connection to everything that makes us whole.

In its final pages, Moments Lost to Time invites readers to see life as a series of intertwined memories, each one adding depth and color to our journey. We come to understand that while moments are fleeting, the impact they leave is timeless. Each experience—whether joyful, challenging, or bittersweet—contributes to the mosaic of our lives, shaping who we are and guiding who we will become. This book serves as both a gentle farewell to what has passed and a warm welcome to what lies ahead. By embracing the ebb and flow of time, we learn to live with intention, finding beauty in each stage of life. Moments Lost to Time ultimately reminds us that every memory, every fleeting moment, and every lesson is part of the ongoing story that we carry within us, an eternal presence that time itself cannot erase. In the end, we are left not with a sense of loss, but with a profound appreciation for the journey—cherishing each moment as a gift, a thread in the ever-weaving tapestry of our lives.

AFTERW ORD

As we reach the close of Moments Lost to Time, we are invited to take a quiet moment to absorb its message, letting its reflections settle within us. This book is not simply a collection of thoughts on time; it is a gentle call to embrace life's fleeting nature with grace and understanding. Through these pages, we've examined the richness of our experiences —the laughter, the tears, the moments we savor, and those we must let go. And perhaps, as we reach this final page, we find ourselves a little more at peace with the nature of time. Time is our most faithful companion, one that moves alongside us whether we recognize it or not. We often wish to hold on tightly to the moments that bring us joy or keep ourselves rooted in times that felt safe and familiar. Yet, as this book reminds us, life is meant to be lived in motion. Just as we cannot cling to yesterday, we cannot live only for tomorrow. We are called to find a delicate balance, a way of appreciating our memories while also allowing them to transform and guide us into each new moment.

Moments Lost to Time has explored the ways in which our experiences shape us, leaving traces that become woven into the fabric of our being. This book has encouraged us to find beauty in both presence and absence, to honor what has passed, and to carry forward the essence of those moments into the future. It has reminded us that while time may take away, it also gives us the wisdom to live with purpose, with compassion, and with an open heart. As we step away from these pages and back into the flow of our lives, may we take with us the insights gained here—the understanding that every moment is both an ending and a beginning, a chance to live with intention and gratitude. Let us be mindful of the moments we are experiencing now, aware of the value they hold, and let us also learn to release them when it's time, knowing they have contributed to who we are becoming. In the end, Moments Lost to Time is a reminder that while our days may be numbered, the impact of each moment is infinite. Each experience, each memory, leaves an indelible mark on us, shaping the journey we are on. And while we cannot hold onto time, we can honor its gift by living fully and embracing the entirety of our journey.

Thank you for allowing these reflections to accompany you. May the insights from this book remain with you, helping you to see the beauty in each passing moment, to cherish your memories, and to look toward the future with a renewed sense of appreciation. Life is precious, and each moment within it is a gift. Embrace it fully, carry it lightly, and allow it to be the quiet teacher that it is.

PRAISE FOR AUTHOR

Ephraim Publishing brings profound depth and insight to the world of literature, crafting works that resonate long after the final page. With a rare sensitivity to the human experiencee, Ephraim Publishing excels at capturing the complexities of time, memory, and existence, inviting readers into beautifully reflective journeys. Their books are both poetic and thought-provoking, encouraging readers to pause, reflect, and reconnect with life's fleeting beauty. In Moments Lost to Time, Ephraim Publishing once again showcases its unique talent for blending rich storytelling with timeless wisdom, creating a book that lingers in the heart and mind. Ephraim Publishing has established itself as a beacon of literary excellence, consistently delivering works that challenge and inspire. Their commitment to exploring the intricacies of the human condition sets them apart in the publishing landscape. With a keen eye for detail and a deep understanding of life's complexities, Ephraim Publishing crafts narratives that resonate across generations. In Moments Lost to Time, they not only illuminate the beauty of transient experiences but also offer readers a comforting reminder of the enduring Impact of our memories. Each page is infused with a blend of eloquence and relatability, making profound truths accessible to all. Ephraim Publishing continues to be a vital force in literature, enriching our lives with stories that invite reflection, foster connection, and encourage us to embrace the journey of existence with open hearts.

- A BLESSING TO HUMANITY, BEST SELLER

www.ingramcontent.com/pod-product-compliance
Ingram Content Group UK Ltd.
Pitfield, Milton Keynes, MK11 3LW, UK
UKRC032033290726
14090UKWH00007B/477

* 9 7 9 8 3 3 0 5 3 4 2 2 7 *